Collins CARE & REPAIR of

Antiques
& Collectables

Collins CARE & REPAIR of

Antiques
& Collectables

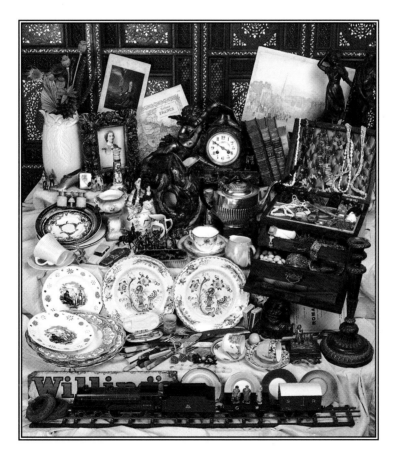

ALBERT JACKSON & DAVID DAY

Collins
An Imprint of HarperCollinsPublishers

ISBN-10: 0-00-712763-4
ISBN-13: 978-0-00-712763-4

ISBN-10: 0-06-113732-4 (in the United States)
ISBN-13: 978-0-06-113732-7
FIRST U.S EDITION published 2006

Printed and bound by Tien Wah Press, Singapore

10 09 08 07 06
9 8 7 6 5 4 3 2 1

Consultants

The authors are grateful to the following consultants for their contributions and assistance.

PAPER COLLECTABLES

Anthony Cross
Warwick Leadlay Gallery,
Greenwich, London
Elizabeth Howard
Bookbinder
Sydenham, London

CERAMICS

Carmen Villacampa
Ceramics restorer
Badgers End, Dorset

TEXTILES

Alexandra Seth-Smith
Textile conservator
Blackheath, London

PLASTICS

John Morgan
Author of
Conservation of Plastics
published by Conservation
Unit of the Museums and
Galleries Commission and the
Plastics Historical Society

TECHNICAL CONSULTANT CONSERVATION MATERIALS

John Lawson
Picreator Enterprises, Ltd.,
Hendon, London

Additional information supplied

A. Bell & Co., Ltd.,
Kingsthorpe,
Northampton
Ciba Polymers,
Duxford,
Cambridge
Cray Pharmaceuticals,
Eltham,
London
ICI Acrylics,
Darwen,
Lancashire
La Ronka,
Hockley,
Birmingham
Percy Reboul,
Plastics Historical Society,
London
Sapphire Products Ltd.,
Nechells, Birmingham
H.S. Walsh and Sons,
Beckenham, Kent

Additional photography

© **EWA** (Elizabeth Whiting & Associates), pages 45, 81, 90, 128, 129. **Paul Chave**, pages 80 bottom right, 108. © **John Morgan**, page 136. © **Neil Waving**, pages 88, 91 bottom right, 109. © **Shona Wood** page 91 top right. © Inklink (**Ben Jennings** Photography) jacket and chapter-opener pages 18–19, 34–35, 52–53, 66–67, 82–83, 92–93, 110–111, 130–131.

The authors and producers are indebted to the following who generously loaned antiques and collectables for photographs.

Stephen and Jane Bull
Glen Chapman
Unique Collections,
Greenwich, London
Jim and Pat Clark
Jacqueline Day
Julian and Ellen Day
Robin and Shirley Harris
Pauline Jackson
Rose Jennings
Christine and Maurice Johnson
John Morgan
Alexandra Seth-Smith
Warwick Leadlay Gallery
Greenwich, London

The authors and producers are grateful to the following companies, who loaned their products and materials as reference and samples for photographs.

Chintex
Stove-Enamelling Glaze
Chintex International
Wraxall, Bristol, Avon

Renaissance
Metal De-corroder
Renaissance
Microcrystalline Wax Polish
Vulpex Liquid Soap
Picreator Enterprises, Ltd.
Hendon, London

Badger Airbrush
Richard Kohnstam, Ltd.
Hemel Hempstead,
Hertfordshire

CONTENTS

CONTENTS

INTRODUCTION

To DETERMINE WHAT MAKES SOMETHING DESIRABLE—and therefore collectable—is difficult, if not impossible. People acquire objects for all manner of subjective reasons, and what one collector judges to be a good investment, another may consider to be an utter waste of money. You can always rely on criteria such as scarcity and condition —and a famous name stamped on the base of a piece of china or signed at the bottom of a picture may be a mark of value, provided that it's genuine. However, you only have to visit a few antique shops and markets to realize that a large proportion of the trade has moved away from what has traditionally been regarded as collectable.

There's no doubt that television programs have had a profound effect on people's attitude toward collecting antiques. By focusing on spectacular "finds" that have netted their delighted owners a small fortune, television has persuaded the average person that it is worth hanging on to heirlooms in case they turn out to be priceless antiques. As a result, fewer items are now making their way into the market, and prices have become inflated. Good pieces are snatched up as soon as they appear, and the apparent scarcity drives prices up even further. With fewer traditional antiques to meet the demand, the trade has inevitably been opening up more abundant seams, drawing out a wealth of items that not long ago would have been rejected by serious collectors. Whereas at one time an object had to be at least 100 years old to be classified as an antique, nowadays the average dealer's stock includes items from the 1940s and 1950s—or even the 1960s—and it appears that almost anything has its price.

Far from being a negative trend, the wider availability and respect for what might be termed "recent antiques" merely serves to widen the opportunities for collectors and amateur restorers. Although rare and valuable antiques have deliberately been excluded, this book covers the widest possible range of collectables from Victorian times to the 1960s; and to make information as accessible and relevant as possible, we have chosen to devote each chapter to a particular material, such as wood, metal, or glass, rather than to specific objects, such as antique clocks or paintings. Consequently, you can look up appropriate techniques and use them for restoring similar pieces from practically any era.

There is a body of opinion that believes amateurs should never be encouraged to restore antiques, for fear that they may do irreparable harm. When it comes to valuable or fragile antiques, we heartily concur. Nevertheless, we take the view that a great many amateurs who are extremely skillful with their hands simply often lack relevant advice and the necessary information in order to make competent repairs to everyday collectables. This book aims to supply that advice and information, gleaned from informed collectors and practicing restorers and conservators.

For some collectors, the excitement of finding a real "gem" is almost as important as acquiring the piece itself and discovering a piece that has eluded them for years may assuage pangs of guilt at having paid a little too much for it. In order to maintain that level of pleasure and excitement, a collection has to grow—and finding accessible and reliable sources of supply is crucial to the process of building up a collection.

Nobody can advise you on what to collect—you are either drawn to it or you're not— but when you are looking around for things that could be of interest, you might consider opting for items that are plentiful and therefore are relatively cheap, rather than trying to compete with collectors who have been active in well-explored fields for years. This doesn't necessarily mean that you have to go in for an area of collecting that is obscure or miss out on types of antiques that are popular—but it does involve doing some research, so that you can back up your own judgment as to whether something is worth collecting, rather than having to rely on catalogs or makers' names.

In any case, most people who are engrossed in their hobby find that research becomes absorbing and highly rewarding. Books and magazines constitute valuable and easily available sources of reference, but nothing can beat the firsthand experience that can be gained by windowshopping and browsing through markets and auction lots where you can handle antiques and examine them closely. In no time at all you begin to get a feel for what is available and whether you are likely to find enough items in restorable condition.

BUYING FROM DEALERS

Whenever possible, any collector prefers to buy items that are in perfect condition, as long as the price is within reason—but the ability to clean and restore damaged antiques is a distinct advantage, especially as even minor flaws can reduce the asking price considerably.

Not all dealers stock damaged pieces, but frequenting a variety of dealers—ranging from high-class establishments to back-street junk shops—gives you a wider choice and also enables you to compare the difference in price between damaged pieces and those in perfect condition.

Get to know dealers who specialize in the types of antiques that interest you. You are unlikely to find bargains, but you will pay a fair going price as the dealer knows the market intimately. In addition, specialist dealers are invariably knowledgeable about their subject and are usually willing to share that knowledge with you—although it helps if you buy something from them from time to time!

Print dealers and small galleries are often a good source of restorable items. The best-quality material is usually mounted for framing or for display in the shop; but the majority of dealers also have folders full of torn and stained prints and other works of art, which they may be willing to sell cheaply rather than pay someone to restore them.

Book prices vary considerably from dealer to dealer. There are far too many subjects for a general dealer to keep track of, so there are frequently bargains to be found. Secondhand books can stay on a dealer's shelves for months, or even years—and a bookseller may be happy to do a deal with you, as long as he or she did not have to pay too much for it in the first place.

Junk shops that stock anything and everything are always worth visiting, but you have to be prepared to trawl through a lot of second-rate material to find the odd gem. Many of these dealers specialize in house clearances, and most of the good stuff is sent off to auctions.

It pays to visit your favorite dealers on a regular basis. You will, of course, see the same stock over and over again, but your persistence will be rewarded when you spot something special that has just come in and can snatch it up before anyone else sees it. Also, dealers soon recognize regular customers and are usually willing to reserve items of particular interest. By frequenting a number of outlets, you will have your finger on the pulse and may be in a position to spot a change in the market—certain items becoming rarer, higher prices being asked for items that once were commonplace—and take advantage of your knowledge to pick up a few bargains.

Most dealers are prepared to haggle. Indeed, some of them anticipate it by setting their prices at a slightly inflated level. A five to ten percent reduction is not unusual, but it depends on what the dealer had to pay for the item. So when he or she tells you that a lower price is not possible, accept it graciously—after all, dealers have to make a living. You will not usually get a reduction for credit-card transactions (except, perhaps, on expensive items), because the dealer has to pay a premium for the service. Most dealers will accept a check if you can guarantee it—but cash is usually preferable, especially for cheaper items or if you are haggling for a reduction.

ANTIQUE MARKETS

Antique markets are mostly weekly events where dealers set up their stalls out in the open air or in halls or centers, but there are also permanent or semi-permanent markets in premises such as large warehouses and converted mills. The better markets are often supported by dealers who run antique shops during the week but bring a different stock to the market, where the lower overheads make for lower prices.

There is very little pressure to buy at markets, allowing you plenty of opportunity for browsing, comparing prices, and examining items at your leisure. Whatever it is you are looking for, you can be sure that there is a stall somewhere that has at least a few items of interest. Antique markets are an especially good source of unusual inexpensive jewelry, simply because it is portable. There are dealers who specialize in precious metals and gemstones, but the majority carry a wide selection of jewelry made from amber, coral, ivory, and other semiprecious materials. You may also come across collectable pieces made from early plastics.

PRIVATE SALE

You can often find interesting antiques by combing through newspaper advertisements or by going to private garage sales. In these circumstances it pays to have a little experience and to be sure of your facts. A private seller may have a highly exaggerated idea of an item's importance and value, perhaps inspired by a similar but rarer item that has been seen on television. However, it may not be appreciated if you start airing your knowledge—so it's usually best to politely decline the purchase and leave it at that.

Jumble sales are similar to buying privately. For a reasonable amount any individual can have a stall for the day and sell anything from discount foodstuffs to genuine antiques. If you attempt to return something that does not meet your expectations, you may not get much satisfaction, as few vendors are likely to be professional dealers.

AUCTIONS

If you are serious about buying and restoring antiques and collectables, keep an eye out for auctions that are held in your hometown or within easy striking distance. They are usually advertised in local papers, and the larger or more important ones may be listed or advertised in specialist magazines.

Auctions are worth visiting even when you don't intend to buy anything. Specialized auctions can be particularly exciting when prices soar because two or more collectors are after a rare piece. However, at many auctions all types of items are up for sale, from furniture to pictures. Job lots are a useful feature of general auctions, where you can buy a box of china, books, or records—almost anything—for a fraction of what you would pay if you bought the individual items from a dealer. Auctions are just the place to buy good quality items at a reasonable price, as well as for picking up bargains—especially if you are prepared to restore them yourself, since any dealer bidding against you has to allow for the cost of restoration on top of what you are prepared to pay.

Try to visit the salesroom on the viewing day (usually the day before the auction). If you wait until the day of the sale, you may not have time to inspect the items carefully—and, as most lots are sold "as seen," it is your responsibility to spot any defects. Carry a small flashlight, a magnifying glass, and a notebook in which you can write down any distinguishing features or marks that you want to check before the sale—another reason for viewing items early.

Buy an auction catalog, giving details of the sale and the price that each lot is expected to reach. Make sure that you know whether the figures are estimates or reserve prices, as that may affect the way that you bid. If an item does not reach its reserve price, it will be withdrawn from the sale; on the other hand, auction lots often go for prices that are far below their estimated value.

Check the catalog carefully for additional charges. Auctions only used to charge the vendors a commission, but nowadays it is common to charge a buyer's premium too—usually ten percent of the hammer price. It is important to take that into account when you are deciding what you want to pay for a piece. Also, remember to allow for any relevant taxes on top of a successful bid.

Catalog descriptions are brief and may only give very few details about the age and provenance (origin). They are often no more than statements of opinion, and therefore carry no guarantee of authenticity. You have to know your stuff if you don't want to go home with a pile of junk—if you have done your research, you will have an advantage over less knowledgeable collectors.

On the day of the sale mark your catalog with the maximum price you are prepared to pay and stick to it. If the bidding intensifies, you may be highly tempted to keep going, and it is all too easy to pay more than you can afford in the heat of the moment. Don't be too disappointed if you fail to acquire the one piece that you had your eye on. This will happen frequently, and just because someone else is prepared to pay more, it does not necessarily mean that the piece is worth it. It is always possible that the successful bidder did not spot the defects you noticed the day before.

The bidding itself couldn't be simpler. The auctioneer makes the running, suggesting the opening bid and then asking for higher bids in simple increments. All you have to do is signify your willingness to pay the asking price by raising your catalog or nodding your head. Don't be deterred by the prospect of having some unwanted item knocked down to you because of an inadvertent gesture. This doesn't happen in real life. In fact, if you haven't entered the bidding at an early stage, you may have to attract the auctioneer's attention by waving your catalog or calling out your bid, because he or she will be concentrating on those who seem the most intent on outbidding each other. If you have been successful, you usually need to call out your name to secure your purchase, though some auction houses give you a number with which to identify yourself. The catalog will give you all the information that you need about what forms of payment are acceptable and when you can collect your lots.

HEIRLOOMS

If you are fortunate enough to have acquired antiques or collectables through an inheritance, have them valued by an expert before attempting any restoration work yourself.

Checking for faults

Once you show genuine interest in a piece, a reputable dealer will invariably point out any defects and should have priced the piece accordingly. However, not all dealers are this scrupulous and, as we have seen, a good deal of auctioneers do not consider it their responsibility to draw your attention to damaged items. In any case, it pays off to train your eye, not only to spot faults and marks, but also to assess whether you will be able to restore a piece yourself or if professional assistance will be needed.

Knowing what to look for will help you over the first hurdle, but only experience can teach you when to invest in expert restoration rather than to do the work yourself. Throughout this book you will find specific advice on when to consult experts—but if ever you are in any doubt, consult a trained conservator or restorer. On the other hand, you may have the view that antiques are bound to show their age and that you are happy to live with the inevitable imperfections. This may be the wisest course of all, as long as you take precautions to prevent any further deterioration.

The following is a checklist of the types of faults you can expect to find, depending on the material from which an antique is made and the care with which it has been handled and stored in the past. No such list can ever be comprehensive, but it will help you detect the most obvious defects—and perhaps avoid the worst pitfalls.

BOOKS AND PERIODICALS

Ideally when you are buying books, you are looking for reasonably clean copies with their bindings intact. You can't always get books wrapped in their original dust jackets, though that would be a bonus.

It is not a good idea to buy books with torn spines or loose covers, unless they are worth the additional cost of professional rebinding. However, you may be able to spruce up dirty or faded book covers yourself, though there is little you can do about heavily stained covers or warped boards.

Flip through a book to check that all the illustrations and photographic plates are in place. If any individual plates are loose, they can be pasted back into a book without too much trouble.

At the same time, look out for signs of insect infestations. Woodworm, for example, have been known to migrate from bookshelves and burrow their way right through a book. This type of damage is impossible to rectify.

It is probably best to reject books or periodicals with badly stained pages, although usually you can remove light soiling. Torn pages and endpapers can be successfully repaired in a number of ways.

PRINTS AND PICTURES

The restoration of oil paintings and other works of art in color should be left to a professional. It is much too easy to destroy or damage a valuable picture if you do not have sufficient experience to identify the medium correctly and then decide on the appropriate course of action. It is therefore the best idea to concentrate your efforts on inexpensive black-and-white prints or drawings done in pencil or waterproof ink.

Don't be put off by soiled or stained prints. If it is necessary, they can be washed in water or a mild solution of bleach. Similarly, crumpled or torn artwork can be repaired but, since it will never be perfect again, the purchase price should be very reasonable.

Collectables that are made from metals are frequently sold in a dirty and corroded state. Sometimes this is because the dealer simply does not have the time to regularly polish them, but the more probable reason is that an experienced dealer knows that some collectors prefer old metalware to exhibit the dull patina of age and cleaning the stock might deter customers. However, it is usually very easy to polish tarnished metals, if that is how you like them.

METALWARE

The one exception may be steel or iron, since they rust when they are exposed to damp conditions. It is possible to clean and stabilize rusting metal, but if the damage is severe, it can only be disguised by filling and painting, which may be detrimental to the value of the piece.

Examine plated metalware for signs of wear. The plating on the high points is often polished away, exposing the base metal. It is possible to have pieces replated, but that often destroys their value as antiques. Before buying chromed collectables, look for signs of blistering, where the corroded base metal is pushing the plating off the surface.

Dents are not too difficult to remove from soft metals, but stay away from deeply creased or folded metal because the damage is likely to be permanent.

Broken metalware can be difficult to assess. A lot depends on how experienced you are at simple metalworking. Depending on the type of metal and the way in which a piece was made, it may be possible to solder or rivet loose components or open seams. But leave any welding to an expert. Some breaks can be mended with glue or discreet mechanical fixings.

It cannot be emphasized enough that you should have antique jewelry valued by an expert before deciding to work on it yourself.

JEWELRY AND SEMIPRECIOUS MATERIALS

Check that there are no loose or missing stones and examine pins, clasps, and other fastenings to make sure that they are solid and in good working order. You can generally repair damaged fastenings by using little more than a pair of padded pliers.

Before buying a necklace, make sure that it is strung onto strong thread that is not about to break, although restringing it is a viable option. If you buy loose beads or pearls, make sure that they are even in size, shape, and color, and that there are enough of them to make a necklace of a reasonable length.

Always examine items that are made from coral, amber, jet, and similar semiprecious materials for signs of previous restoration and to ensure that there are no obvious chips or deep scratches.

Bone and ivory were frequently used to make handles for silverware, manicure sets, and sewing equipment. If this type of handle comes loose, it can be cleaned up and reglued.

China and pottery damage easily, so look at a piece from all angles to spot any chipped rims and cracks. Hairline cracks can be difficult to detect unless they are dirty. If you hold porcelain up to the light, you may have a better chance of noticing a crack. And if you place the piece in the palm of your hand and tap it gently with your fingernail, the porcelain will ring if it is solid.

CERAMICS

Mending cracks and chips is relatively easy. Even reassembling broken china is not too difficult, once you have practiced the appropriate techniques. But it takes a level of dexterity and some artistic ability to replace missing components such as cup handles or a hand on a porcelain figure.

Crazed glaze (fine cracked glaze) is something most collectors accept, as long as it has not become ingrained with dirt. Given time, it is possible to soak out most ingrained soiling and other stains.

Try to detect old repairs for two reasons. First, a restored piece should cost you less than one that is in perfect condition; and, second, if you wash a restored piece in hot water, it may disintegrate. You can't miss old riveted repairs, but rivets can prove to be tricky to remove if you find that you need to make a more satisfactory repair.

Surface decorations may be worn away in patches—often because plates, cups and saucers, and other tableware have been stacked carelessly or have been washed in a dishwasher. It is never easy to restore worn decorations. Either decide to live with it or practice on something that is less desirable until you have developed the necessary skills to restore it.

GLASSWARE It is practically impossible to make invisible repairs to broken glassware. The best that you can expect to achieve is a sound and safe repair; but it won't stand up to close scrutiny, nor can you expect to put the item back into use.

Examine glass decanters for old wine stains and white watermarks, as they can be difficult to remove. Also, look carefully to make sure that the stopper matches the style and decoration of the decanter.

Colored-glass windows—leaded lights—are relativley specialized antiques. Except for hand-painted panels, leaded lights have little appeal as collectables; but they make attractive glazing either *in situ*, as originally intended, or hung in front of clear-glass windows. Check old leaded lights for broken or buckled leadwork and for cracked or missing quarries (the individual pieces of colored or textured glass). They are all repairable, but only by a skilled restorer. On the other hand, it is relatively easy to fill in the gaps around loose quarries, to stop them from rattling, and to clean up dirty glass and leadwork.

You will often come across old mirrors that are "fogged" or speckled with small, brown stains. These defects are the result of moisture penetrating the silvered backing. There is nothing you can do to rectify these faults, except to have the affected mirrors stripped and resilvered by a specialist—which tends to detract from the value of genuine antiques.

WOOD When it comes to wooden collectables, it is often the surface finish that is damaged rather than the wood itself. White watermarks and other surface blemishes can be disfiguring—but they are rarely impossible to rectify, although occasionally you may find that you have to resort to stripping and refinishing the whole piece.

Dents, splits, and deep burn marks require more work, because you need to treat the wood itself; but unless the damage is very severe, you can generally make a passable repair.

Veneered pieces are especially vulnerable. Glance across a veneered surface to check that there are no blisters that will need flattening and inspect the edges of any veneered panel to see if the veneer is chipped or lifting. Also check to see if there is any loose or missing marquetry or inlay.

Always be on the lookout for signs of recent woodworm. A mass of small clean holes and pale dust are signs of recent activity. There is no reason why you should not buy a wormed piece provided that it is basically sound, but it is imperative that the infestation is treated early on before it spreads to other items made from wood.

TEXTILES

Antique textiles constitute a vast field of collectables that need careful preservation—including old clothes, which many people enjoy wearing. The best advice is to do as little as possible, except for repairs that will prevent further deterioration. As you probably don't want to be seen wearing tatty clothes, examine potential purchases for signs of deterioration, especially in those areas that receive the most wear, such as collars, cuffs, and sleeve elbows. Unless you are buying the garments for a collection of historical costumes, it is probably the best to look for wearable items in better condition.

Also check that all the necessary fastenings and buttons are present and securely attached.

Restoring antique textiles demands slightly different techniques from those normally used for mending modern textiles. It is vital that the methods you use do not put additional strain on what may be weakened fabrics. Holes and tears can be patched successfully, but don't take on the restoration of very fragile or large-scale textiles.

In some cases it is possible to wash or dry-clean soiled textiles. But some old stains—especially perspiration stains—cannot be removed, even by experts.

Usually it is the best to reject textiles that show signs of moth infestation. Unless the dealer can guarantee that the textile has been treated professionally, it is not worth the risk of introducing infestation to your collection.

CARPETS AND RUGS

Since carpets and rugs are generally used as floor coverings, one expects to see signs of legitimate wear and tear. Apart from minor repairs to worn side cords and fringes, there is not much that an amateur can safely do to restore a worn carpet or rug. So, if you detect holes, splits, or missing fringes, you need to agree on a price that allows for the cost of professional restoration. If you find a rug that appears to have been folded for some time, examine it carefully to make sure that the fibers have not been damaged along the crease lines.

PLASTICS

Not all antique plastics have the same characteristics. Some are brittle and are more likely to crack or shatter. Others will bend without breaking, but may exhibit stress marks along the crease. Again, some plastics are more susceptible to fading than others, and some are more easily scuffed or scratched. Accurate identification is the key—and it will pay to study the chart on page 137, so that you are aware of the most likely defects when hunting for plastic collectables.

POTENTIAL ENEMIES

With the exception of fire, the greatest risks to anything made from paper are moisture and high humidity. Moisture not only causes actual physical damage in the form of warping and puckering, it can also encourage mold growth and staining. Dampness can also attract insects that feed on organic glues and paper. Generally, a dry but relatively cool environment suits paper products the best. With too much heat, paper becomes brittle.

It is also important to protect paper from airborne dust and pollution. Fine dust gets absorbed into the paper, and larger gritty particles act like an abrasive. Even more harmful are invisible pollutants: industrial emissions and traffic fumes can attack and discolor paper.

Long-term exposure to ultraviolet light is detrimental, too. Daylight, the main source of ultraviolet radiation, causes color pigments to fade and eventually makes the paper disintegrate.

Careless handling and inappropriate storage are possibly the most common causes of physical damage—especially to items that were considered worthless until somebody started collecting them.

Although it is possible to do a great deal to slow down the deterioration of paper collectables that have suffered in the past, the best possible course of action is to protect them from adverse conditions. Advice on storage and mounting will be found throughout this chapter.

PAPER COLLECTABLES

The considerations that determine whether a piece of paper is collectable—and therefore worth preserving—have little to do with the material itself. In fact, two very similar pieces of paper can be worth vastly different amounts of money, depending on what has been applied to them and by whom. A drawing or engraving may have artistic merit to commend it. Another scrap of paper may owe its survival to sentimental attachment; or the fact that it is a charming and colorful piece of ephemera may have saved it from being discarded. Documents and photographs are frequently prized for the information they contain or because of their association with a famous person. Clearly, although conservation aims to preserve the paper itself, the real objective is to ensure the survival of what is on it.

To a large extent, this is likely to affect your approach to conservation. It is important, for example, to decide whether legibility and access to information are more important than aesthetic considerations. And most people would prefer to live with a stained picture, rather than risk losing the image itself.

There are three golden rules. Be clear about your objectives; make sure you know what medium you are dealing with; and proceed with caution. If you are in any doubt, seek the advice of an expert before tackling the restoration yourself.

CLEANING PICTURES

The true value of a watercolor, drawing, or print may be measured in money, artistic merit, rarity, age, or personal association with a place or person—but what should matter more to you as a restorer is whether you can successfully improve its condition or appearance. Old pictures, like all antiques, have a quality that develops with age. Slight discoloring of the paper, stains, and muted colors are all clues to a picture's provenance and can add a lot to its character. Without them, you might just as well hang a reproduction on the wall—so hesitate for a moment and ask yourself whether cleaning will enhance the picture or may in some way detract from its appearance.

Your next decision is whether you can safely undertake the work yourself. This will mostly depend on how much the picture is worth and on what medium has been used to create it. Valuable pictures in need of restoration should always be handed over to an expert, so should fragile drawings in chalk, pastels, or charcoal. You are on fairly safe ground with black-and-white prints, as long as you are sure that they are not photographic reproductions; but obtain an expert's advice before doing anything to colored artwork. Don't abrade pencil and never wash ink drawings unless an expert has assured you that the ink is waterproof. Finally, don't attempt to restore artwork that is on very thin or delicate paper.

Dry methods

Before resorting to drastic measures, always try erasing ,marks in case they are merely on the surface of the paper. Overall treatment with document cleaner (see right) will increase the contrast of an ink drawing or print, but if you are left with stubborn marks or dirty patches, try removing them with a pencil eraser (see page 29). You may be able to pick off tiny specks with the point of a sharp knife but be careful not to pluck the surface of the paper. The use of document cleaner or a pencil eraser is safe for most types of artwork—but not for pencil drawings.

Using document cleaner

Document cleaner—powdered eraser—is ideal for cleaning grubby artwork. Its action is so gentle that it can be safely used on hand-colored prints and watercolors, as long as you do not rub too hard; but never be tempted to use document cleaner on pencil drawings. Available from bookbinders' suppliers, it comes in an open-weave bag that you squeeze to distribute the powder onto the paper.

To avoid rubbing dirt into the paper, brush any surface dust off the artwork with a soft brush. Holding the picture firmly on a non-slippery tabletop, sprinkle document cleaner onto the surface and gently rub the bag over the soiled paper with overlapping circular strokes. Be careful to avoid tearing or creasing the paper as you reach the edges.

Washing pictures

If dry methods are not successful, you could try washing the picture in cold water. Even if it does not entirely eradicate any ugly staining, washing will at least have the advantage of pulling out natural acidic impurities, which eventually destroy old paper.

The process is usually safe for black-and-white prints, but don't soak colored pictures or drawings that are made with watersoluble inks. The same applies for any picture that is signed with ink, but you will find that pencil signatures are usually impervious to washing in water.

Distilled water should remove the majority of stains, or at least reduce them to an acceptable level. Adding a little salt to the water may help pull out blood and wine stains, but remember to rinse the picture thoroughly in freshwater. Don't use hot water, as it tends to set stains permanently.

Until you become experienced at washing pictures, don't attempt to soak large prints in water—they become heavy and difficult to handle. The same is true of badly damaged pictures, which have a tendency to disintegrate when they become wet. Washing thin and delicate paper is also a task that is best left to an expert.

Foxing

Small brown spots known as "foxing" are caused by spores growing on damp paper. If it is necessary, foxing can be dispelled by immersing the print in a mild bleach solution.

Equipping yourself

You can improvize to a certain extent, but you will find washing and drying prints is easier—and more efficient—if you purchase a few specialized products. They are sold by bookbinders' or conservators' suppliers, most of whom offer a mail-order service.

Archival support fabric, made from nonwoven polyester, enables you to handle wet paper safely and facilitates air drying by natural circulation. For this you also need a drying rack that is made by stapling fiberglass netting across a softwood frame. If this purpose-made netting is unobtainable, try using fine plastic netting from a garden store.

You can wash paper in any large plastic bowl or bathtub, but it pays to buy a flat tray that is designed for washing photographic prints. Make sure that the tray is large enough to allow your prints to lie flat under the water.

1 Immersing the print in water
Cut a piece of support fabric to fit the bottom of the tray, making sure that there is enough to support the print on all sides. Fill the tray with cold water and gradually immerse the supported print by sliding it beneath the surface from one end.

2 Rinsing regularly
After around 20 minutes carefully remove the support fabric and print, refill the tray with freshwater, and reimmerse the print. Repeat the process four or five times with 20 minute intervals.

3 Leaving the print to dry
After the fifth rinse (or earlier if you get a satisfactory result) take the print and its support out of the water and lay them on your drying rack. At this stage it doesn't matter if the print does not dry completely flat, because you will probably need to size the paper anyway (see page 22). If you prefer, wait until the print is almost dry, then press it flat between two sheets of clean blotting paper, using a warm iron.

Water staining
Accidental soaking draws dirt into the fibers of the paper. Prints in this condition often benefit from being washed in cold, distilled water.

Bleaching prints

If after it haas been washed in water your print still exhibits a disfiguring stain, you could try immersing it in a weak solution of bleach. However, bleaching artwork is a controversial subject. Some authorities believe that amateur restorers should never attempt bleaching—in fact, some would suggest that bleaching should not be recommended under any circumstances, because of the possible long-term effects on the paper fibers. To be safe, it's best to only bleach inexpensive black-and-white prints; anything else should be tackled by an expert. Ensure that the paper is thoroughly soaked in cold water before you put it into a bleach solution.

Make a solution of bleach and water in the same tray that you use for washing artwork. The professional restorer would mix four teaspoons of Chloramine T in one pint (0.5L) of cold, distilled water. This bleach is only available from specialist suppliers. Alternatively, use a household "sterilizing fluid"—a mild bleaching agent and antiseptic used, among other things, to sterilize babies' bottles. Mix the sterilizing fluid with four parts water.

1 Bleaching the print
Wearing tight-fitting vinyl gloves, lower the print, backed with archival support fabric, into the bleach solution. Keep an eye on the print and, as soon as the stain disappears, carefully lift out the print, pour away the bleach, and refill the tray with freshwater.

2 Rinsing the print
Leave the print to soak for 20 minutes before replenishing the water. Repeat the process five times, as described for washing artwork, then leave the print on a drying rack to dry naturally.

Damaged prints
Torn prints can be repaired with starch paste or document-repair tape. Badly damaged artwork may need to be relined (see page 24).

SIZING PAPER

Paper that has been bleached and soaked in water is relatively weak and benefits from a coat of "size." Make a suitable size by mixing half an ounce (10g) of ordinary gelatine in one pint (0.5L) of water.

Applying the size
Lay the washed and dried print face down on a clean sheet of paper. Coat the paper generously with size, using a wide, soft brush to cover the print evenly. Blot off the excess size and leave the print on a drying rack to dry naturally.

REPAIRING PICTURES

Repairing creased or torn pictures is relatively straightforward with modern conservation-grade materials, as long as the damage is minor. It is vital to ensure that the image on the paper will not be harmed or obscured by the processes.

Flattening creased drawings and prints

Once paper has acquired a distinct fold, it can be difficult, if not impossible, to rectify. However, dampening and pressing a pencil drawing or a black-and-white print might minimize the effect. Don't try this with colored work or ink drawings unless you have been assured that the medium is entirely waterproof. Similarly, avoid spraying any picture that was previously glued to a backing board, in case the water reactivates the adhesive.

Spraying and pressing the paper

Lay the creased picture face down on a clean sheet of damp blotting paper and moisten the back of the print or drawing with a spray bottle filled with distilled water. Moisten a second sheet of blotting paper and lay it down on top of the print.

Place all three sheets of paper between two stiff boards and weight them down with heavy books. Alternatively, put the boards in a press until the paper has dried.

Eliminating a scored line or indentation

A sharp edge or point pressed into paper leaves a deep impression. If the image itself has been scored, seek the advice of a professional restorer. But if the indentation is across the border of the picture, you can use an artist's brush to paint hot water along the scored line.

Let the water soak in for a few minutes to allow the paper fibers to swell, then lay blotting paper over the mark and rub it down with a bookbinder's bone folder or tacking iron (see page 31).

Repairing torn artwork

The methods for repairing torn artwork are the same for any graphic image that is drawn or printed on paper—but, since recommended archival paste is made with water, the usual restrictions apply to artwork that is made with watersoluble materials. Nevertheless, as long as the damage does not extend across the image itself, careful repair work should leave the picture unharmed.

Similarly, although conservation-grade adhesive tapes and tissues make excellent reinforcements when they are applied to the back of a picture, it is not advisable to apply them across the image itself, even though these materials are practically invisible when they are rubbed down.

Mending a simple tear

Often a tear in relatively thick paper has overlapping, feathered edges, which are easy to reconnect with starch paste. Use a specialized bookbinder's paste or buy conservation-grade wallpaper paste. Both types of pastes are reversible and are guaranteed to not stain the paper or promote the growth of mold.

Use a pointed artist's brush to apply the paste sparingly to one feathered edge, then hold both torn edges together. Wipe off any excess paste with a clean paper tissue, cover the repair with silicone-coated release paper, and rub it down with a bone folder.

Reinforcing a repair

A glued repair should be strong enough without any further reinforcement. But if the overlap is minimal or the paper was cut, leaving no feathered edges at all, apply a special self-adhesive paper tape to the back of the picture. Archival document-repair tape is made with reversible acrylic adhesive that, unlike the glues used for ordinary stationery tapes, will not deteriorate and stain the paper. When it is rubbed down with a bone folder, document-repair tape is almost invisible—and you can buy a slightly yellow tape that is close to the color of old paper.

Relining a badly damaged print

Simply regluing the torn edges may not be enough to repair a print that has been ripped in half. A more professional approach is to reline the picture by pasting handmade Japanese tissue paper to the back. It is not easy to achieve perfect results, but considering that a badly damaged print is probably worth very little, you are not risking a great deal. Nevertheless, it is advisable to have the picture valued before you proceed.

1 Preparing the tissue
Tear or cut the Japanese tissue paper two inches (50mm) larger than your print on all four sides. Lay the paper onto a sheet of glass and moisten it with a spray bottle. Tape the moist paper to the glass with gummed brown-paper tape and leave it to dry.

2 Pasting the print
Brush starch paste onto the back of each half of the print and lay them onto the tissue paper, carefully aligning the torn edges. Lay a sheet of silicone-coated release paper over the print and gently rub it down, using a soft cloth pad. Peel off the release paper and leave the print to dry.

3 Trimming the picture
Once the print and tissue paper are dry, trim around the taped edges with a very sharp knife and lift the relined print off the glass.

MOUNTING AND STORING PICTURES

Display and store your collection of pictures within the normal living areas of your home, where it is easy to maintain a relatively dry, clean, and stable environment. But don't hang framed pictures in direct sunlight or above a direct source of heat, such as a radiator or a fireplace.

BACKING BOARD
HINGE
TAPE
MOUNTING BOARD
ARTWORK
WINDOW MOUNT
GLASS
FRAME

Framing pictures

Ready-made picture frames are rarely suitable for displaying antique prints, drawings, or watercolor paintings. There is no guarantee that they are made from conservation-grade materials—and inexpensive, frameless versions, comprising a sheet of glass clipped to a stiff backing board, offer little protection from dust and airborne pollution.

Whether you make your own frames or order them from a professional framer, it pays to ensure that only acid-free boards and paper are used to mount your pictures. Conservation-grade materials are widely available from art supply stores and conservators' suppliers

The style of the frame is a matter of personal taste. But if you are in doubt, choose a slim, simple molding for the frame and off-white or cream-colored mounting board that will not detract from your picture.

All artwork on paper should be framed behind glass (nonreflective picture glass is an option, but not essential). Some collectors prefer to use transparent polycarbonate or acrylic sheeting. These materials are marginally safer than glass and can be treated to protect your pictures from ultraviolet light. However, plastic glazing can acquire a static charge that makes them unsuitable for chalk, pastels, or charcoal drawings.

Thin double-sided hardboard, sealed with an acrylic varnish, supports the picture from behind and protects it from any damage.

Cutting mounts

Most prints, drawings, and watercolors are sandwiched between two sheets of mounting board—one with a window cut through it to display the artwork (it also maintains a space between the glass and the picture). When measuring the window mount, allow a generous border all around the image. Based on convention, a relatively wide border beneath the picture makes for a visually balanced mount. The window itself, which is usually cut with beveled edges, should allow enough room for the picture to "breathe" and should never conceal a plate mark (the impression left in the paper during the printing process) or the artist's signature.

Mounting the picture

The picture should never be pasted onto a mounting board directly. Instead, hang it from Japanese-paper hinges attached with starch paste (see page 23). Paste another strip of paper across each hinge to reinforce it.

Inserting the backing board

Once you have assembled the frame, along with the glazing and mounted picture, secure the backing board in the frame rabbet with nonrusting brads or metal "points." Finally, seal the gap around the backing board with gummed brown-paper tape to protect the picture from dust and insects.

Storing pictures in folders or boxes

If you are a serious collector of prints or drawings, it will be impossible to display your entire collection in wall-hung picture frames. In this case, store your pictures in shallow boxes that are made from acid-free cardboard. These purpose-made boxes—available in a wide range of sizes—have metal-reinforced corners and a front flap that drops down to provide easy access to the contents once the lid is removed. Either make a simple paper folder for each picture or interleave them with acid-free tissue paper.

CONSERVING OLD PHOTOGRAPHS

Like other prints on paper, photographs need protection from light, dust, and physical damage. In addition, the chemical composition of the photographic emulsion makes them particularly susceptible to pollution and fluctuating levels of temperature and humidity.

As a general rule, keep your photographs in a relatively cool environment that is free from dust and moisture. Try to store them away from exterior walls and painted or varnished surfaces that might release harmful fumes. Never use a damp cellar or a dry, dusty attic for storing photographs.

Safe storage

The traditional photograph album is still one of the best ways to store old photographic prints. It enables you to view your collection easily and quickly without having to touch any of the photographs, and it will prevent them from fading as a result of exposure to light. It is possible to buy albums that are made entirely from conservation-grade materials. You may also want to purchase transparent polyester corner mounts that are chemically stable and guaranteed not to cause long-term deterioration of the emulsion.

Storing individual photographs

An album may not be suitable for storing an extensive collection, nor if you want to be able to compare or check the information that is printed or written on the reverse.

You can wrap one or two photographs in acid-free tissue paper and slip them into a strong envelope, but make sure that the envelope is not made with glued seams that might react with the photographic emulsion.

File a larger collection in strong archival-quality cardboard boxes, with each photograph enclosed in an acid-free, nonalkaline paper wallet—or, even better, in a transparent polyester sleeve that allows you to handle the print without touching its delicate surface. All these materials are available by mail order from conservators' suppliers.

Displaying photographs

Display old photographic prints in wall-hung frames, in a similar way to other artwork printed on paper (see page 24). However, be especially careful about the boards you select for your mounts. Most so-called acid-free cardboard is "buffered" with an alkaline substance to prevent acid contamination. These are perfectly adequate for most archival purposes, but research suggests that buffered boards in close contact with photographs may be harmful in the long run. Unbuffered materials should therefore be chosen in preference.

Reproducing old photographs

One way of avoiding possible harm to a fragile or rare photograph is to make a copy—the original can then be stored safely, and the reproduction displayed without risk. Even badly creased, stained, or faded photographs can be improved and enhanced without having to retouch the original. Many professional photographers act as agents for this highly specialized service.

Mending torn photographs

You can make a passable repair to a torn photograph by using starch paste (see page 23). It won't repair cracked or flaked emulsion, but gluing the torn paper may prevent further damage to the photograph. Paste the torn edges together, as described on page 23. If it is necessary, reinforce the back of the print by pasting a narrow strip of Japanese tissue paper over the repair; alternatively, use archival document-repair tape.

Restoring photographs

If you have rare or valuable photographs that need restoring, have the work done by an expert who is able to identify with certainty the exact base and chemical process that was used for a particular print. However, you can clean and repair your own family photographs—which may not be valuable in monetary terms but are worth preserving for future generations.

Cleaning prints
Cleaning an old print with water is likely to cause the emulsion to swell. However, you can remove fingerprints, mold, and some ink marks from the surface of old photographs with a cleaning fluid that is available from conservators' suppliers. Spray the fluid onto a clean lint-free cloth and gently rub the print using circular strokes. The fluid should dry instantly, without leaving a residue.

RESTORING BOOKS

Being mostly made from paper, books suffer from exposure to moisture, dust, insects and the effects of physical abuse. But because the paper is bound between cloth- or leather-covered boards, the restoration techniques that have already been outlined for pictures and printed ephemera have to be adapted to suit the peculiar construction of books.

How books are made
Books are printed on large sheets of paper that are folded and trimmed to make sections of leaves, which are then sewn together to make the basic book block. The spine—the sewn edge of the block—is reinforced with a strip of open-weave fabric known as mull, and sometimes with transverse strips of cloth tape. Decorative headbands are sometimes glued across the top and bottom of the spine.

The mull and tapes form hinges or "joints" between the block and the book cover, which is made by covering thick strawboard or millboard with cloth or thin leather. Relatively thick endpapers, glued to the inside of the cover, conceal the joints and form a flyleaf at the front and back of the book.

Many books are wrapped in a decorative paper dust jacket. You should always attempt to preserve a book's dust jacket, regardless of its condition, since it is invariably of value to collectors (see page 32).

Restoring books yourself
A lot of restoration strays into the realms of bookbinding—a highly skilled activity that requires specialist knowledge and practice to perfect. Old books that are in very poor condition are therefore likely to require the services of a professional. This is especially true of volumes with decorative or fragile leather bindings—and always consult an expert about the restoration of rare or valuable books. However, cleaning and making minor repairs to ordinary secondhand books is definitely within the capabilities of the amateur who is willing to purchase a few specialized tools and materials. You can buy all the equipment you need from any bookbinders' or conservators' supplier.

SECTIONS

MULL

BOOK BLOCK

TAPES

HEADBAND

ENDPAPER

BOOK COVER

BLOCK

FLYLEAF

ENDPAPER

DUST JACKET

BOUND BOOK

Cleaning books

It is important to dust your books regularly. As well as reducing the risk of dust particles getting in between the leaves, it provides an opportunity to inspect your collection for signs of mildew and harmful insects. To avoid the possibility of introducing spores and insect eggs to your collection, dust recent acquisitions thoroughly before putting them on your bookshelves. Temporarily remove loose dust jackets before dusting books.

Cleaning cloth book covers

Although dusting removes loose surface dirt, it will do nothing for grubby covers that have lost the protection of their dust jackets. Cleaning the cloth cover will not restore the book to its original pristine condition, but it can spruce up a dowdy book by reviving the color of the cloth. Unlike water (which may damage metallic-foil blocking), a proprietary book-cloth cleaner is safe to use on any cloth-bound book.

1 Applying book-cloth cleaner
Put a little cleaner onto a ball of cotton wool and rub it across the cover, including the spine, using overlapping circular strokes. Turn the cotton ball over as it becomes dirty.

2 Buffing the cover
Leave the cover to dry for a few minutes, then buff the cloth with a clean soft-bristle shoe brush. This should give the cover a nice, even color.

Dusting a book
Holding the book tightly closed between your forefinger and thumb, use a soft-bristle paintbrush to dust off the head, brushing from the spine outward. Wear a gauze face mask when you are cleaning very dusty books.

Dealing with mildew

If you discover mildew growing on the cover of one of your books, check your collection for other affected copies and put them aside to dry out thoroughly. This can be achieved the best by standing the books upright with their leaves fanned open in a dry, well-ventilated area. Check your bookshelves to locate and rectify the source of the moisture that caused the contamination.

Once a book is perfectly dry, take it outside to brush off the powdery deposits. There is very little that you can do yourself to fix warped boards or stained cloth covers—but if the damp conditions have left the cover looking dull, though basically clean, then you can revive its appearance with white microcrystalline wax polish. The same process will restore some of the color to a faded spine.

Applying microcrystalline wax
Dip a ball of cotton wool into the wax then, after dabbing the pad on a piece of scrap paper to remove any excess polish, rub the wax sparingly onto the book cover, using circular strokes to spread it out evenly. Be careful not to smear the wax onto the pages. A few minutes later buff the cover with a soft-bristle shoe brush or lint-free cloth pad.

Cleaning endpapers and flyleaves

You will often find that the flyleaf or title page of a book is inscribed with the names of previous owners, dedications, dates, and occasionally the signature of the author or illustrator. Some people attempt to erase such marks if the names are not well known, but it is a pity to lose these reminders of a book's past history. It makes more sense to only remove unsightly scrawls and dirty patches that truly spoil the book's appearance.

Using document cleaner
Rubbing with document cleaner (see page 20) is the safest method for cleaning grubby endpapers—but be careful if you want to preserve anything that is written in pencil. Document cleaner can be safely used on printed and coated endpapers, as long as you do not rub the paper vigorously.

Support the open book to avoid straining the joint and gently rub outward from the center of the flyleaf to make sure that you don't crease or tear the paper. Carefully brush the powdered debris from the book before you close it.

Stained and foxed books
Books that have been stored in damp conditions or subjected to flooding are often disfigured by watermarks or exhibit brown speckling known as foxing. Both can be eradicated by washing or bleaching the paper (see pages 21–22)—but since neither method is practical with a bound book, it is probably best to not buy stained or foxed copies unless you are prepared to keep them in that condition.

Erasing underlining

Although not impossible, it can be difficult to erase penciled notes or underlining from the pages of a book, since the paper is likely to have taken an impression. Don't buy books that have been underlined with ink or felttip markers—such marks cannot be removed without damaging the paper.

Using pencil erasers
Try using a good quality soft eraser made from white vinyl. In addition to the usual small blocks, these are available as refills that fit a retractable stylus—ideal when you need greater accuracy. Alternatively, use a soft, puttylike eraser that you can knead into whatever shape is convenient and reshape as it becomes dirty.

Whatever type of eraser you choose, support the open book and rub with short, straight strokes from the spine toward the edge of each leaf (don't use circular or reciprocal strokes, which could crease the paper) and work diligently to avoid erasing any print. Stippling with a softened putty eraser will often remove dirty patches without having to rub.

Cleaning plates

Document cleaner will remove dirt and smears from the surface of illustrative plates (avoid using erasers that tend to leave streaks on shiny, coated paper). Be extra careful when you are cleaning plates—you may find that they are just "tipped in," or lightly glued into the book.

Repairing damaged books

Don't be deterred from buying a book just because it has broken joints or the endpapers are missing. This type of repair is a professional bookbinder's stock in trade, and you may find that the cost of restoring the book is perfectly affordable. You certainly don't need specialist skills to fix dog-eared pages or to replace a loose frontispiece or mend a torn page—all that is required is care and patience, and you can practice on books of little worth before you tackle something that you care about.

You will have to judge for yourself whether it is advisable to clean the paper before repairing it. You don't want to trap dirt under a strip of pasted tissue paper or tape, but there is always a risk that you could make the damage worse by rubbing the paper with document cleaner or an eraser. The condition of each book will be a guide to the best course of action. It is generally accepted that it is best to leave cleaning the cover until last.

Some of the techniques for repairing books can also be used for restoring magazines, comic books, and other printed ephemera.

Flattening folded corners
Some readers have a habit of folding the corner of a leaf to mark their place. Also, the pages of books that are printed on thin paper often have dog-eared corners as a result of careless handling or storage.

Rubbing with a bone folder
Open up all the affected corners, using the tip of a bookbinder's bone folder. Place a piece of cardboard under the damaged leaf and lay a strip of thin paper on top of it, then flatten each corner by rubbing down along the crease with the folder. The crease will always show, but the leaf will at least remain flat.

Inserting a loose plate
A scrupulous dealer may have already made a note of missing plates. If not, before buying a book, look at the list of illustrations in the front pages. Alternatively, the number of illustrations may be printed on the title page.

Loose plates are not a problem. They can be reinserted easily—and this is something that you should do as soon as possible, before their edges become scuffed and dirty. If you are not sure where a plate should be inserted, check whether its intended location is printed in the margin.

Individual plates, including the frontispiece, are usually tipped in (glued along one edge) and simply require repasting. With more modern books, pairs of plates tend to be wrapped around sewn sections—in which case, you need to tip both plates back into the book to make an effective repair. Use a reversible conservation-grade PVA adhesive, which is available from bookbinders' suppliers.

1 Applying adhesive
Lay the loose plate face down onto a sheet of clean white paper. Mask the back of the plate with another sheet of paper, leaving a thin strip exposed along the plate's inner edge. Paint the adhesive sparingly onto the plate's exposed edge, brushing outward from the mask.

2 Inserting the plate
With the book open, use a finger and thumb to align the corner of the plate, while holding the glued edge away from the leaf below. Carefully rub down along the glued edge, then lay a strip of silicone-coated release paper into the hinge and close the book.

Leave the release paper in place until the adhesive has set.

Repairing torn leaves and endpapers

There are several options for repairing torn books. Your choice will depend on whether the repair needs reinforcing and whether you are willing to buy specialized equipment.

A water-based paste is cheap and simple to use and may be all that is required to make an adequate repair. Applying conservation-grade self-adhesive tape will be a stronger repair and is practically invisible—even on printed pages.

Heat-set tissue paper is a good alternative to self-adhesive tape and can be torn to whatever shape is required to cover irregular tears. However, you need a special electrically-heated tacking iron to set the adhesive.

Pasting torn paper

A simple, overlapping torn edge can be repaired with paste (see page 23). Sandwich the repaired page between two sheets of silicone-coated release paper, close the book, and leave the paste to dry.

A properly glued repair should not require reinforcing, but if the book is to be used frequently or the repair is vulnerable in any way, it helps to cover the repair on at least one side with document-repair tape (see page 23) or tissue paper.

Using document-repair tape

Wash your hands before handling adhesive tape. Choose the tape that is most similar to the color of the page and tear it into a narrow strip with feathered edges. Apply the strip of tape to the page, lay a piece of paper on top, and rub it down with a bone folder to expel trapped air. Place a piece of cardboard beneath the repair, then use a steel ruler and knife to trim any excess tape flush with the edge of the leaf.

Reinforcing with heat-set tissue paper

Coated tissue paper, with a heat-setting acrylic adhesive on one side, produces a repair that is barely discernible. The adhesive is protected with a carrier sheet, which should not be removed until you are ready to make the repair.

Tear the tissue paper to roughly match the shape of the damage and lay a piece of the carrier sheet on top. Rub down the tissue paper with the broad tip of a hot tacking iron.

If you want to make a repair without pasting the edges first, begin by laying a protective sheet of paper on the damaged leaf, then flatten the fibers along the torn edges with a bone folder. If you don't do this, a slight ridge may be apparent underneath the tissue. Apply tissue paper to both sides of the leaf.

Reinforcing weak or torn folds

Illustrated books sometimes have foldout maps and diagrams that are in need of attention—especially if the paper on which they are printed has become brittle with age.

Reinforce a weak fold by applying document-repair tape (see left) or a strip of heat-set tissue paper (see above) to the back of the illustration.

If a diagram has torn into several pieces, it is best to reline it with handmade Japanese tissue paper (see page 24)—but only if you can be sure that water is not going to harm the printed surface. You can make a similar repair with heat-set tissue paper, although a heated press is needed in order to set a large area.

Removing a tipped-in diagram

Folded diagrams or maps are often tipped into old books. If you intend to reline a torn diagram, you need to remove any pieces that remain pasted in, so that you can make an effective repair. Holding down the adjacent page with the palm of your hand, peel back the glued edge with a straight pull. Once you have repaired the diagram, paste it in place, as described for inserting a loose plate (see opposite page).

Repairing a cracked hinge

The joint between the cover and the book block is an obvious weak point. Endpapers are therefore often the first place to show signs of wear along the hinge line. As long as the mull and reinforcing tapes are still intact, you can restore the appearance of a joint by regluing the ragged edges where the endpaper has cracked. Quick action can save printed or illustrated endpapers, which become difficult to repair once the entire joint fails completely.

1 Applying glue to the crack
Carefully peel back the torn edges, so that you can brush out any dust that may have penetrated the crack. With a narrow pointed paintbrush, sparingly paint conservation-grade paste into the crack, making sure that the paper is evenly coated.

2 Closing the crack
Use the blade of a blunt table knife to lift and press the cracked hinge back into place, aligning the torn edges exactly. Wrap a barely damp, lint-free rag around your finger and press down the glued edges, while wiping off any smears of paste.

3 Pressing the book
Fold a strip of silicone-coated release paper and place it into the joint, then close the book and rub down the joint with your finger. Place the book between two stiff boards, aligning them with the joints to avoid crushing the spine. Place a heavy weight on top and leave the glue to set overnight.

Protecting dust jackets

Dust jackets are especially vulnerable to damage, which is probably why so many secondhand books are sold without them. If you are lucky enough to acquire a book with an intact dust jacket, it pays to protect it with a transparent sleeve that will keep it clean and prevent any further deterioration.

For rare books you may want to buy purpose-made jacket protectors—but as an inexpensive alternative for less valuable copies you can adapt the bags used by florists for wrapping bouquets of flowers. Before sleeving the jacket, smooth out any creases and realign any torn edges. The sleeve or bag may hold a slightly damaged jacket together without further treatment, but repair a badly torn jacket with heat-set tissue paper (see page 31) or document-repair tape (see page 23) before sleeving it.

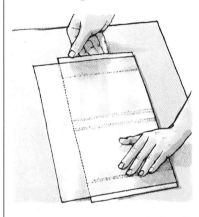

1 Making the sleeve
Cut the sealed end off the bag to make an open-ended sleeve that is approximately one inch (25mm) shorter than the overall width of the dust jacket. Slip the jacket into the sleeve, until it fits tightly against one folded edge and projects an equal amount from each end of the sleeve.

2 Folding the sleeve over the jacket
Place the sleeve and jacket face down on a table. Align a long, straight ruler with the top edge of the dust jacket and, while holding the ruler down firmly, fold the sleeve over the jacket. Remove the ruler and rub down the crease.

3 Wrapping the book
To ensure that the sleeved jacket fits tightly, begin by wrapping it around the spine of the book, then place the book flat on a table with the spine facing you. Open the book and fold in one jacket flap. Close the book, turn it over, and fold in the other flap.

MAGAZINES AND PERIODICALS

Since they lack the protection of cover boards, magazines, comic books, and other periodicals are extremely vulnerable to physical damage. You can clean them and repair torn or creased pages using methods that are similar to those described for bound books. What sets most periodicals apart from sewn books is that the sections are held together with metal staples; consequently if they have been stored in damp or humid conditions, the staples are likely to have rusted, staining the surrounding paper. If the paper is becoming fragile, then your only option is to remove the rusted staples and sew the periodical with linen bookbinding thread.

Three-hole sewing
There is little you can do about rust staining; but if the paper has torn around the staples, close up the hole and reinforce it with a torn strip of document-repair tape before sewing.

1 Starting at the center
Punch a small hole through the exact center of the hinge and two more that are equidistant from the center. Start by pushing a threaded needle through the central hole from inside the magazine.

2 Passing back through
Pass the needle back through the top hole and, skipping over the central hole, pass the needle out through the bottom hole.

3 Tying off
Now pass the needle back through the central hole, cutting off the thread to leave two long tails on the inside of the magazine. Tie these in a knot, enclosing the length of thread running down the center of the hinge. Finally, trim off the tails.

Storing magazines and comic books
Keep individual magazines and comic books in transparent sleeves made from polyester or polyethylene. File your sleeved collection in acid-free cardboard boxes.

GOLD AND SILVER

Although they have many other uses, gold and silver are primarily associated with fine jewelry. The quality and color of these metals—whether used on their own, or together, or combined with other precious or semiprecious materials—make any item made from them special. Gold is very soft and therefore easily damaged (how easily depends on its purity). Silver is harder, though still relatively soft compared with most other metals. Items made of solid gold or silver are expensive because of their metal content. To reduce the cost and weight, some pieces are made hollow. Also, as a cheaper alternative, gold and silver are often plated onto metals of lesser value. Rolled gold and silver, fused to a base metal and rolled into a thin sheet, can usually be identified by their lack of markings and relatively light weight. Electroplate (see page 38), which has a thin, chemically bonded film of precious metal, was developed in the mid–nineteenth century and largely superseded rolled gold and silver.

GOLD STANDARDS AND MARKS

For commercial use gold is alloyed with other metals (usually silver or copper) to improve its strength or modify its color. The quality of gold is represented by its karat value, which is the proportion by weight of pure gold to the alloyed metal(s). Pure gold is 24 karat. The current gold standards are 22, 18, 14, and 9 karat, although 15 and 12 karat were also produced in the past. In North America the "k" of karat, together with the maker's mark, helps identify the gold's origin. However, in Great Britain, karat is spelled with a "c." Genuine British pieces are stamped with a "carat" number, maker's mark, hallmark, and date letter.

METALS

The practical and aesthetic properties of metalware are highly appreciated, but when it comes to anything more than light cleaning, metal is mostly viewed as a difficult and unsympathetic material only to be worked by specialists. Yet shabby objects made from this versatile material can be usefully restored with basic craft skills.

Metals or their compounds are extracted from ores or metal-bearing minerals and then either processed into various grades of a single metal or combined with other metals to form a range of alloys that have different properties.

It is often difficult to identify metals very precisely, but it is usually possible to recognize the general type by its color, weight, and hardness. The object itself is also a clue, as the characteristics and value of the various metals tend to lend themselves to particular uses.

Color is generally the most useful guide, although this will vary according to whether the surface is polished, tarnished, or corroded.

GOLD AND SILVER JEWELRY

Have valuable, precious–metal jewelry cleaned and maintained by a professional jeweler. Gold does not tarnish, and plain pieces do not need much more than a rub with a soft cloth or chamois leather to keep them bright. Remove light tarnish from silver with a proprietary long-term silver cloth.

Dirt in the form of grease from soap or makeup can mar the appearance of a piece that is intricately shaped or set with gemstones, making further cleaning necessary.

CLOSED SETTING

OPEN SETTING

Checking the setting

If the piece is set with stones, examine it closely. Gemstones may be held in a closed or an open setting. With a closed setting, the stone is enclosed in a recess that is formed in the mount. Sometimes a foil backing is placed behind the stone to enhance its color and brightness. This type of setting should not be exposed to moisture, nor should enameled pieces.

An open mount gives access to the back of the stone, which makes cleaning easier. As long as the stone is not porous, simply wash it in warm, soapy water.

Remove rings, or wear rubber gloves to protect them, when doing domestic washing.

Using a dip cleaner

Use a commercial dip to clean small or intricately detailed jewelry that is not affected by moisture. Dips are available from jewelers in a range of types for cleaning gold, silver, and gemstones. Use a separate dip for each type of material.

Following the maker's instructions, place one item at a time into the dip solution for the prescribed duration (usually not more than one minute). Remove the piece from the dip and gently brush the surface with the small soft brush that is provided as part of the kit. Rinse it thoroughly in clean water, then dry with a soft cotton cloth or chamois leather.

Cleaning open settings

Clean large pieces of open-backed jewelry, such as a brooch, with a solution of mild liquid dishwashing soap. For better-quality jewelry use conservator's liquid soap and warm water (one part soap in ten parts water), plus a few drops of ammonia. Use a plastic bowl placed on the sink drainer. Do not work directly over the sink, as you risk losing pieces in the drain. Remove the dirt with an old toothbrush, then rinse it in clean warm water and dry by blotting with a soft cotton cloth or paper towel.

Cleaning closed settings

Since trapped moisture could damage the setting, use methylated spirit or specialist isopropyl alcohol, instead of soap and water, to loosen dirt. Apply the spirit carefully with a cotton bud and wipe off the residue with clean cotton buds. For light soiling, use dip-cleaner fluid applied with a cotton bud. When it is dry, carefully buff with a chamois leather.

Chains

Wearing a gold or silver chain regularly will keep it bright. However, it may be necessary to remove grease and dirt from time to time. For solid chains use a dip cleaner or wash them in liquid soap and warm water or a mild solution of liquid dishwashing soap.

Do not immerse a hollow chain in liquid: if it is made from plated metal, trapped moisture may cause corrosion. Instead, pin each end to a soft board panel that is covered with cotton cloth. Remove the dirt from the outstretched chain with a soft brush that is dampened with dip cleaner or a mild soap solution. If it is necessary, turn the chain over. Blot the moisture and loosened dirt from the chain with an absorbent tissue, then polish it with a soft cloth.

Simple repairs

In most cases repairs to precious metal jewelry are the best when they are done by a jeweler, and it is not advisable to attempt them yourself. However, there are some basic repairs—requiring only simple tools—that you can undertake yourself on items that will not be unduly harmed. (See also pages 54–57.)

Storing jewelry
Keep regularly worn gold or silver jewelry in a cloth-lined tray that has separate compartments or in individual velvet-padded boxes or fabric pouches that are available from jewelers and specialist suppliers. This ensures that the soft metal will not get scratched or dented and prevents necklaces and bracelets from becoming tangled. For long-term storage wrap each piece in acid-free tissue paper. Rolling chains in the tissue paper makes them easier to handle. Keep jewelry in a stable environment, away from excessive heat.

Chain rings
Jump rings are used to form a closed loop at one end of a chain and to link a clasp or a bolt ring at the other end. Both jump rings and bolt rings can be damaged by wear or distorted by force. If they are beyond repair, you can buy gold or silver replacements in various sizes.

Fitting a jump ring
Always open a jump ring by twisting the butting ends sideways, using two pairs of small pliers. Wrap the jaws of the pliers with adhesive tape to prevent them from marking up the metal. Open the ring no more than is necessary to loop it into position, then close it by twisting the ends back together.

Replacing a bolt ring
Bolt rings are attached in a similar way to jump rings. They are available in a range of sizes and come with an attached open or closed ring for attaching it to the chain.

Loose finger rings
Loose finger rings can easily get lost. If you prefer not to have a loose ring permanently resized by a jeweler, you can reduce the internal diameter by attaching a ring clip.

Buy a clip that fits the width of the ring band and simply spring it into place.

SILVERWARE

Silver is an important commercial metal that has been used for a wide range of domestic items. Generations of silversmiths have produced beautiful pieces, which by virtue of their craftsmanship and use of material have become desirable to collectors. And yet it is still possible to discover silver items, such as matchstick cases, cups, and pots, that have not been recognized for what they are. This is because, if left unpolished, silver will tarnish in the presence of a sulfurous atmosphere, first turning yellow, then dark blue or black. To confirm that a piece is silver, look for the maker's mark that is stamped in the metal.

English silver is the easiest to identify, since a system for standardizing the quality was introduced in the thirteenth century, consisting of a series of marks giving details of the assay office (hallmark), quality, date, and maker. These marks may be accompanied by a number indicating the parts of silver per thousand. Continental Europe and North America did not adopt such formal regulations for control of the silver trade, although the town and maker's marks were used and can be a useful guide. However, silver marks are not always clear or genuine—and careful analysis, aided by reference books, is advisable.

Sheffield plate
Invented in 1742, Sheffield plate is a thin, rolled sheet material, consisting of silver fused to a copper backing. One or both sides may be plated. The edges were often covered with silver or covered with silver wire, sometimes making identification difficult. Worked like solid silver, it was used for a range of flat and hollow domestic silverware. Although Sheffield plate was not generally marked, nineteenth-century items may have simulated silver marks.

Electroplated silver
The electroplating process, introduced in 1820, enabled cheap silverware to be produced by electrolytically depositing a thin film of silver onto preformed base metal pieces. Electroplated nickel silver (EPNS) is often used for silverware and other items of tableware; an alloy of nickel, copper, and zinc, it is sometimes referred to as German silver. Britannia metal (EPBM)—an alloy of tin and antimony—is also used.

Silver gilt
Silver electroplated with a thin covering of gold is known as silver gilt. It is used for plating hollowware, jewelry, and decorative items. It should be treated in the same way as electroplated silver.

Cleaning silverware

Polish silver as little as possible, since overenthusiastic cleaning can cause more harm than not cleaning the metal at all. Hollowware, such as teapots and jugs, and tall, narrow pieces, such as candlesticks, can be distorted or broken by rough handling, while repeated polishing of silver-plated pieces can wear through the surface and expose the base metal.

Handling silverware
For flatware, such as dishes and trays, cover the table with a soft cloth to cushion the piece. When you re polishing hollowware, always support it well. Do not press down on lightly made pieces, nor hold them by their handles or spouts. Instead, hold the object against you, supporting it from underneath with one hand. Wear an apron and, in order to prevent tarnishing as a result of fingerprints, wear cotton gloves. Specially treated gloves are available for cleaning and polishing silver.

Washing silverware
Regularly used silver usually needs no more than routine washing to maintain its shine. Tarnished silver should be washed before it is polished, in order to remove any traces of dust or grit that could scratch the surface. Where it is possible, remove items such as teapot or coffeepot knobs that are made from other materials, before cleaning. Using a soft cloth, gently wash one piece at a time in a plastic bowl that is filled with a solution of warm water and liquid soap (see page 36) or liquid dishwashing soap. Use a soft brush to get the dirt out of crevices. Rinse it in clean, warm water and dry it immediately with a soft cloth; you can also use a hair dryer for drying intricate pieces. Buff the metal with a proprietary silver cloth.

Removing tarnish

There are a number of cleaning products that are available for polishing silver: impregnated cloths and wadding, silver foams, silver creams, and liquid polishes. Choose one that is chemically formulated to give long-term protection—every time a piece is polished some silver is removed, and a long-term polish will avoid the need for frequent cleaning.

Apply the polish with a soft cloth, following the manufacturer's instructions. Work it in gently in a circular motion, turning the cloth when it becomes dirty; then buff the surface with a clean cloth. To clean decorative work, use a soft brush, cotton buds, or wadding. When clean, wash the polished metal to remove any traces of the cleaner, then dry it thoroughly, giving it a final rub with a soft cloth. Be very careful with plated silver, and as an alternative use a silver dip (see below).

Electrochemical dip

Chemical dips soften or remove tarnish from silver, copper, and brass by an electrochemical process. For small items use a commercial silver dip or swab the piece with the dip solution.

To make your own dip for cleaning large objects, line a plastic bowl or bucket with around three feet (1m) of aluminum foil, or use an old aluminum pan. Tie a length of string to the piece and place the silverware in the container in contact with the foil or pan.

Wearing vinyl gloves, make up a solution of one cupful of washing soda (sodium carbonate) to 3½ pints (2L) of very hot water. Make enough to cover the item completely and pour it carefully into the bowl. A chemical reaction will cause the solution to bubble as the tarnish is removed.

Lift the piece out frequently to monitor its progress. When it is clean, remove it from the dip; wash and dry it immediately, and then polish it. For very heavy tarnish, it may be necessary to repeat the process.

Another alternative is to use a commercial cleaning plate. This will produce the same electrolytic reaction, but cooking salt is used in the hot water. There is also a tarnish-removing product for silver in the form of a packet that contains all the that are materials required—you simply add water.

Do not use a dip for cleaning items that are composed of a mixture of materials—including ones with weighted bases such as candlesticks—nor treat separate pieces made from different metals in the same dip solution. Strip old lacquer before cleaning it (see page 41) and do not use a dip for artificially patinated items.

Cleaning niello

Niello is a type of silverware that is decorated with engraved designs filled with a black compound. Particular care is needed when cleaning niello, as the piece will be damaged if the compound is removed. Never use a dip, but lightly clean the surface with a long-term silver polish to reveal the design.

Storing silver

Wrap pieces in acid-free tissue paper to protect the surface from abrasion and atmospheric pollution. To avoid condensation problems, place them in ventilated polyethylene bags and store them in a cool place. Cloth wraps and bags that are impregnated with tarnish inhibitor are also available for protecting silverware.

Copper and brass

Polished copper cooking pots, pans, kettles, and jelly molds demand to be displayed around the walls or surfaces of any kitchen. In fact, for most of us copper and brass epitomize the comfort of old-fashioned country kitchens.

It is surprising that copper was used for cooking pots, since it can contaminate foodstuffs that react with it—which is why copper vessels are usually lined with a coating of tin. Nevertheless, it does absorb and hold the heat easily and evenly, and copper pans are still favored by chefs today.

Unlike copper—which is a pure metal and has a pinkish color—brass is an alloy of copper and zinc, and its attractive bright yellow coloring can be mistaken for gold. There are, however, many different types of brasses, some of which contain a higher proportion of zinc, as well as other metals such as tin, lead, and nickel. Brass has good working and casting properties and considerable strength. It is used for a variety of domestic items, such as lamps, vases, coal scuttles, and ornaments, as well as for household fittings, such as doorknobs, fingerplates, hinges, and locks.

Cleaning copper and brass

Atmospheric pollution will tarnish both copper and brass. Old polished copper takes on an attractive warm-red patina that is the best when it is preserved by not overcleaning it. Uncared-for copper, on the other hand, tarnishes to a dirty, dull brown, and if it is exposed to moisture, it may develop a green coating of verdigris. Such corrosion is sometimes desirable for copper outdoors, as the oxide becomes stable and the weathered appearance looks most attractive. Brass tarnishes to an unattractive dull, greenish-brown. Brass is traditionally polished to a bright finish, but it looks best when it has mellowed to a rich golden yellow.

Washing the metals
Before polishing copper or brass pieces, first wash them in a solution of warm water and liquid soap (see page 36) or mild liquid dishwashing soap. Use a soft brush for working into the moldings. Rinse it thoroughly in clean water, and dry it well with a soft cloth.

Polishing
Wearing protective gloves, use an impregnated polishing cloth to polish lightly tarnished copper or brass. Always use a separate cloth for each metal. Treat heavier tarnish with a commercial copper-and-brass cleaner, applying it with a soft cloth and working with a circular motion. Remove the cleaner and polish the surface with a clean, soft cloth.

Dealing with corrosion
Use a chemical dip (see page 39) to soften stubborn tarnish. For small spots make a paste of cooking salt and white vinegar and apply it to the mark with an artist's bristle brush. Try to avoid runs, as the cleaned brass will turn slightly pink. Rinse it off after ten minutes, and repeat if it is necessary. Finally, wash and dry the item thoroughly, then polish to it restore the color.

Waxing copper and brass
A simple and effective way to reduce tarnishing and the need for regular polishing is to periodically apply a thin coating of microcrystalline wax, using a soft cloth.

Lacquering metal

You can eliminate the need for harmful regular cleaning of ornamental copper, brass, and silverware by applying a clear lacquer. Brush-on and spray-on metal lacquers are available. Lacquers can preserve the finish for many years in normal household conditions. Work in a warm, well-ventilated, dust-free room or workshop.

1 Preparing the surface
Polish the metal—but not with a long-term cleaner, as that can affect the bonding of the lacquer. Wash the piece to remove all traces of polish and dry it thoroughly. Wearing cotton gloves, wipe the surface with methylated spirit to remove oily fingerprints.

2 Applying the lacquer
Using a soft, fine brush, apply the lacquer quickly and evenly. Two coats are better than one, as there is a tendency for a heavy coating to form a puddle in moldings. Turn the piece as you go, working systematically to ensure that all surfaces are coated the first time. Leave it to harden overnight before applying the second coat.

Spraying lacquer
Lacquers can be thinned out and applied to fine detailed work with a spray gun. You can also buy aerosol cans for finishing copper and brass. These are quick to use and avoid brushmark problems, but can produce a heavy spray. Follow the manufacturer's instructions carefully.

Removing lacquer
Worn or missing lacquer creates a patchy appearance. Before the metal can be polished, the old lacquer must be removed. If shellac has been used, remove it with swabs of methylated spirit or acetone for cellulose lacquers. Use paint stripper if these fail to make an impact, as well as for removing other types of lacquers. When cleaning an item made from a mixture of materials, make sure that you apply solvents to the appropriate surfaces only. Clean a small area at a time.

ORMOLU

Ornate gold-colored pieces, such as candelabras, clock cases, and fancy metal mounts on the corners of furniture, are likely to be made from gilded cast brass or bronze, known as ormolu (French for ground gold). True ormolu has a thin coating of gold over the base metal, but some examples are simply fine-polished, lacquered brass, while others are gilded spelter (see page 44).

Ormolu should not be polished, as it is easy to remove the surface gilding. Wear on the high points of moldings is acceptable and should not be retouched. Have fine or corroded ormolu restored professionally.

Cleaning ormolu
Clean ormolu with great care. Where it is possible to remove mounts, take notice of their position and fixings. If the gilding is in good condition, it may be possible to clean the surface. For light soiling remove any dust, then clean and protect the surface with an application of microcrystalline wax. For heavier soiling try gently removing old furniture-wax accretions by using white spirit applied with cotton buds. Follow with a warm solution of conservator's liquid soap (one part soap in ten parts water), to which a few drops of ammonia have been added. Apply the solution with well wrung-out cotton wool swabs, then wipe it with swabs that are dampened with clean water. Dry it thoroughly and buff with a soft cloth. Apply a protective coating of microcrystalline wax.

Fixing a loose handle

Old copper and brass vessels often have handles attached with copper or brass rivets. Wear can cause the handles to loosen. If a rivet is missing, buy a matching replacement to fit the hole. Solid rivets are made in copper, brass, aluminum, and mild steel. Dome-headed rivets (known as snap-head rivets) are usually used, but countersunk or flat-head rivets may also be used. You can buy rivets from metal and tool suppliers or from specialist suppliers; if you only need one or two, you may be able to obtain them from a local blacksmith or hardware store.

Tightening rivets
If the rivets are in place and are not badly worn, try to secure the handle by spreading the rivets in their holes.

Depending on the shape of the vessel, support each rivet on the inside with a metal stake or hammer that is held in a vice. Make sure that the handle is held tightly against the pot. Using a ball-peen hammer, strike the rivet to compress it in the hole; then, if necessary, use the ball end to reform the head by carefully tapping it in a circular sequence.

1 Replacing rivets
For a snap-head rivet cut the length so that one and a half times the diameter of the shank protrudes through the hole. Hold the waste end in a vice and cut the rivet to the correct length with a small hacksaw.

To form a smooth dome-headed rivet, you will need a rivet set, two rivet snaps, and a ball-peen hammer.

RIVET SET

RIVET SNAP

RIVET SNAP

RIVET SNAP

2 Fixing the rivet
Place the rivet through the hole from the inside. Support the rivet head in one snap that is held in a vice. Place the set over the rivet shank and strike it to force the parts together. Remove the set and hit the end of the rivet to spread it.

3 Shaping the rivet
Roughly shape the dome with the ball of the hammer. Then place the second snap over the head of the rivet and hammer it down to produce the final

Removing dents in copper and brass

Light dents in copper and brass vessels that are caused by normal use can be accepted as part of their character. However, a large dent in a prominent part can disfigure the form. Have the work carried out by a specialist if the piece is valuable or if the dent is creased or likely to be difficult to remove.

1 Using a sandbag and a mallet
For simple shapes, such as a plain bowl, use a leather sandbag and a wooden bossing mallet, both of which are available from tool suppliers. You can make your own sandbag from sewn canvas filled with silver sand. Form a hollow in the sandbag to support the bowl and tap out the dent from the inside.

2 Using a stake
Make a wooden stake from a tightly-grained hardwood, such as beech, with the end shaped to a curve slightly tighter than that of the inside of the dented bowl or vessel (this method can be used for other forms besides bowls). The end of the stake must be smoothly finished. Place the bowl or vessel over the stake and tap out any unevenness on the outside, using a soft-headed mallet.

Soldering a seam
Use a large electric soldering iron for making a joint in relatively thin metal, to repair an item such as a copper pot. The larger the "bit," the more heat it can hold. Heat the iron; when it melts the solder easily, it is ready. Dip the bit in flux to clean it, then apply a little solder to "tin" the tip. With the components temporarily clamped or wired together, apply the flux to the joint; then heat it with the iron. Hold the iron in contact with the seam at one end and apply the solder; at the right heat it will melt and flow into the joint. Run the iron along the seam, followed by the solder, to form a continuous joint. Avoid using too much solder, as an unsightly excess can be difficult to remove without damage. Allow the metal to cool, then clean off the flux.

Soldering copper and brass

Soldering is a method of connecting metals using a molten alloy with a melting point that is lower than that of the metals to be connected. When it cools, it forms a permanent bond. This process may be roughly divided into two categories: soft soldering and hard soldering. Soft soldering uses a low-melting point alloy of tin and lead that only needs local heat from a soldering iron or a blowtorch. It is not particularly strong, but it is simple to use and requires minimal equipment. Its silver-gray color is readily identifiable on old copper wares and tinplate.

Hard soldering—otherwise known as brazing or silver soldering—uses solders that have a high melting point. It produces a strong joint for brass and silverware. The metal has to be at or near red heat; and to generate and maintain such high temperatures, a gas blowtorch and a firebrick hearth are required. Silver solder alloys are available with a range of melting points for assembling complex pieces. Repair work of this kind should be left to a specialist.

Soft-solder fluxes
Metal that is to be soldered must be clean. A flux also has to be applied in order to protect the joint from oxides, since oxides resist solder and would weaken the bond. Two types of fluxes are commonly used, active and passive. Acid-based active fluxes are corrosive and must be washed off after use. They are more effective for soft-soldering copper, brass, tinplate, and steel since they help clean the surfaces. Non-corrosive passive fluxes, sold as resin paste or in resin-cored solder wire, are purely protective, so the parts need to be thoroughly cleaned.

Fixing separate parts
When a component such as a handle becomes detached, it should be possible to refix it with a "sweated" joint—when both parts have been coated first with solder. If the faces of the old joint are not well covered, clean the surfaces, apply a flux, and recoat or "tin" them with a thin layer of solder. When they have cooled, apply more flux, then position and clamp the parts together. Apply heat with a soldering iron or blowtorch until the solder flows in the joint, then leave it to cool. Wash away all traces of flux prior to polishing it.

BRONZE

Bronze is a particularly good metal for casting, which is why it is so widely used for statues and molded ornaments, intended for both indoor and outdoor use. Bronze is basically an alloy of copper and tin, but its properties and color can vary with the addition of lead or zinc. Old bronze develops a highly-prized, rich brown patina, which should always be preserved. Some pieces may be artificially colored to reproduce this effect. When it is placed outdoors, bronzes develop a greenish-blue patina.

Caring for bronzes
Bronzes should not be overcleaned, as this will ruin their color. Simply dust the surfaces regularly to prevent the buildup of dirt. Use a soft brush to remove any dust from crevices. Never wash bronze unless you are sure that it is not patinated spelter (see below), as risk damaging the coloring. You can wash a piece that is made entirely from bronze with a liquid soap solution (see page 36), applying it sparingly with cotton wool swabs. Alternatively, use a mild liquid dishwashing soap. After washing, dry the piece thoroughly. Treat dull bronzes with microcrystalline wax to clean and revive the surface. Apply it with a soft cloth, then buff it with another clean, soft cloth. Indoors, keep bronzes away from damp conditions to prevent any corrosion.

Exterior bronzes
Outdoors, bronzes develop a stable greenish patina that needs little attention, unless it is subjected to heavy industrial pollution. To protect the metal, wash the surface with a solution of liquid soap and warm water (see above). Leave it to dry, then seal it with a thin coating of microcrystalline wax applied with a soft bristle brush. Rewax from time to time.

Bronze corrosion
Bright green powdery spots may be an indication of bronze disease that is caused by a reaction of copper salts within the metal. Clean it with metal decorroder, then rinse it with clean water, dry thoroughly with a hair dryer and finish with microcrystalline wax. If the problem persists, consult a specialist.

Spelter
Spelter was used in the mid nineteenth century as a cheap substitute for cast bronze statues and ornaments. An alloy of zinc and lead that has good casting properties, it was either patinated to look like bronze or decoratively painted or gilded. To check whether a bronze-colored casting is made from spelter, make a small scratch on the underside. If the exposed metal appears silvery, then the casting is not genuine bronze. Clean and maintain spelter the same way as bronze.

PÊCHEUR

PÊCHEUSE

PEWTER

Pewter is perhaps best known in the form of period domestic flatware, tankards, and candlesticks, but it also became fashionable in the early twentieth century for art nouveau pieces. Old pewter was primarily an alloy of tin and lead, but antimony, copper, or bismuth were sometimes used in place of lead. Examples of the finest plate pewter, which contained no lead, may bear an "X" quality mark. Maker's marks may also be found on early pewter. Britannia metal, developed in the late eighteenth century, was a high-quality form of pewter that was widely used for silver-plated items. It looks like silver when it is polished, but it dulls to a light gray color. Modern pewter, which is an alloy of tin and antimony, has a tarnish-resistant finish that resembles dull silver.

Maintaining pewter

Old pewter generally has a stable dark gray patina that needs little attention. If it has a high proportion of lead, then the color is likely to be particularly dark. Handle pewter carefully, as it is a soft metal and so can easily be dented or scratched. Do not use coarse abrasives on old pewter, since they will damage the patina. However, some collectors prefer to keep their pewter brightly polished.

Maintain the condition of pewter by removing dust and buffing it occasionally with a soft cloth. Wash soiled items in a solution of liquid soap and warm water (see page 36), rinse thoroughly and dry with a soft cloth.

Do not store pewter in an atmosphere that contains organic acids—for example, inside an oak cupboard or in boxes that are constructed from man-made materials containing a high percentage of glue. Wrap individual pieces in acid-free tissue paper and place them in ventilated plastic bags.

Corrosion on old pewter may cause small lumps to appear. If the condition is not stable, have it treated by a specialist.

Reshaping pewter
Pewter is soft enough to be manipulated by hand. If you have a hollow vessel that has been slightly deformed so that it is no longer perfectly round, squeeze it carefully with both hands to ease it back into shape.

Restoring buckled flatware
For flatware with a lightly buckled rim, work the edge between your fingers and thumbs to straighten it. If you find that the metal is too hard to work with your fingers, place the rim on a thick pad of newspaper and gently manipulate it with a wooden roller, as used for wallpapering.

LEAD

Until the middle of the nineteenth century the majority of children's toys were simple, locally made items. But with the Industrial Revolution and the development of mechanized production, it became possible to mass produce metal toys at an affordable price. Manufacturers soon discovered that there was a lively demand for representational toys depicting all types of subjects—including soldiers, animals, boats, trains, and automobiles.

Antique toys that are made of lead or tinplate—or, later, die-cast zinc—have become highly collectable; and examples that are in good condition can collect high prices. It is unusual to find an old toy in mint condition, but a well-used toy showing normal wear and tear is generally preferable to one that has been stripped and restored.

Lead castings
Lead is a very soft and heavy metal that has excellent casting properties. In addition to toy making, it was used for much larger work, such as garden statues and architectural fittings. When it is first cast, it has a bright silver color, but this soon oxidizes to a stable light gray patina, which usually weathers well and needs little attention. Lead is toxic if it is ingested, so always wash your hands after handling it.

Lead soldiers

At first lead soldiers were cast as simple "flat" figures. Solid cast figures, which were more animated in form, then took over, until manufacturers began to produce cheaper, hollow cast models. The soft nature of lead makes it difficult for a toy to remain in perfect condition, and parts easily get bent or broken. However, although lead is very malleable, it is not advisable to try to straighten out bent pieces since there is a risk of fracturing the weakened metal. Do not repaint old lead soldiers, as that will considerably reduce their value.

Mending broken parts
It may be possible to reattach a broken part of a hollow-cast figure by reinforcing the break with a wooden peg or short piece of solder wire glued into the hollow section. If it is necessary, ream the hole with a drill bit to make it symmetrical. Try the parts to see if they fit, then apply a clear, general-purpose glue into the holes, attach the peg, and assemble the joint.

Recasting missing parts

Solid cast soldiers were sometimes made with separate plug-in heads. If the head of a soldier is missing, it may be possible to cast a replica from another head. The replica can then be glued into place and painted with enamel. To make a casting, you will need cold-cure silicone rubber for the mold and low-melt casting alloy for the figure. Various cold-cure molding rubbers are available from specialist craft suppliers to suit the size and complexity of the molding. Choose a firm-setting rubber for hand casting low-melt metals.

1 Making a two-piece mold

Make a wooden box to contain the rubber mold. Make it a generous size to ensure that the sides of the mold are thick. Apply a release agent of thinned petroleum jelly to the inside. Half fill the box with soft clay and press the head of the lead soldier into it so that it is half buried. Also, turn or carve a wooden cone and press it halfway into the clay at one end. This will create a reservoir for the molten metal. Impress cone-shaped indentations into the clay around the head in order to form location pegs. Thoroughly mix the silicone rubber and catalyst together, following the manufacturer's instructions, then fill the mold box and leave the rubber to set.

2 Making the second half

Turn the mold box over and carefully remove the clay. Clean the model head, wooden cone, and exposed rubber. Apply a release agent to the surfaces and fill the second half with rubberm as before. When the rubber has set, remove the box, split the mold, and remove the head and cone. Using a scalpel or linocut tool, cut a channel from the reservoir to the head spigot; also cut air vents from the bottom of the molding to the top of the mold. The vents prevent air locks from forming when the metal is poured.

3 Casting the metal

Dust the two halves of the mold with talcum powder, then clamp them together. Choose a suitable casting metal from the range that is offered by specialist suppliers. An alloy with an extra-low melting point is the best for hand casting.

Using a flat-bottomed ladle, melt the metal on a stove. Pour the liquid metal into the mold until it is full, then leave it to cool.

4 Attaching the head

When the molding has set, remove it and trim off the sprue (waste metal) with a sharp knife. Try the head to see if it fits and trim the neck spigot if it is required, then glue it into place with a clear, general-purpose adhesive. Paint the new head to match.

CASTING METAL SAFELY

* ★Always read and follow the manufacturer's instructions.
* ★Place the mold on a metal tray.
* ★Wear leather gloves and strong protective clothes.
* ★Protect your eyes with goggles.
* ★Wear a face mask.
* ★Do not work near children or animals.
* ★Do not cool hot metal with water.
* ★Wash your hands after handling lead.

TINPLATE

Tinplate is composed of a thin, rolled steel sheet that is plated on both sides with a thin rust-proofing layer of tin. Tin is a soft, nontoxic, durable metal that does not corrode easily but forms a stable light gray oxide. As a plating material, it is typically used for tinning food, as a lining for copper items, and for tinplate used in various lightweight pressings. In its solid form it has been used for domestic flatware and hollowware. It is also widely used as an alloy with other metals.

Tinplate toys

Until the Victorian period toys were mostly made out of wood, but with the development of tinned steel in the mid nineteenth century, manufacturers began to mass produce lightweight pressed-tinplate toys. These flourished in Germany, America, and Great Britain, with a number of companies producing a variety of toys, including clockwork horse-drawn carriages, boats, trains, and automobiles.

Early examples were assembled with solder and painted by hand. An improved method of assembly for mass production featured a series of slots to hold tabs that were bent to lock the parts together. This allowed the components to be finished individually before being assembled. Later in the nineteenth century the introduction of offset lithography enabled toy makers to print detailed designs onto the tinplate before it was pressed into shape.

Cleaning tinplate toys

It is best to clean tinplate toys as little as possible, since the surface finish is very thin. Dust them occasionally with a soft cloth or a soft artist's brush for parts that are awkward to reach with a cloth. As long as the tin plating is intact and the decorative finish is solid, you can remove grime with mild liquid dishwashing soap or a warm solution of liquid soap (see page 36), applied with a soft cloth. Be careful not to allow water to get inside the toy and dry the surface thoroughly. To remove greasy marks, wipe the surface with white spirit. Apply a thin coating of microcrystalline wax to protect the finish.

Treating rust

Since the steel is plated with such a thin covering of tin, exposure to atmospheric pollution for long periods is likely to cause the base metal to corrode. Rust is difficult to eliminate successfully, so it is the best idea to place valuable items in the hands of a specialist. If there is light rusting on less treasured pieces, you can try treating the problem yourself.

1 Removing loose rust
Using a miniature power drill with a brass wire brush, carefully remove the loose rust. Be extremely careful not to damage the painted areas. Degrease the surface with white spirit, then wipe it dry.

2 Applying rust remover
Brush on a coat of proprietary metal decorroder to remove and slow down the corrosion. Check the surface periodically, and when it is clean, carefully wipe off the rust remover with a cloth and clean water. To brighten the metal, rub the surface with a mildly abrasive chrome polish. Wipe the surface and dry it thoroughly, then seal it with a coat of microcrystalline wax. Repainting the toy is likely to reduce its value.

Fixing a broken tab
Metal that is bent will become brittle or "work-hardened," and if it is continuously flexed, it will eventually break. If one of the tabs holding the parts together has broken off, you can make a replacement. Using tin snippers, cut a strip of tinplate from a suitable can to the required width and length. Clean the faces of the tab and inside the toy, which may have to be dismantled. Next, solder the tab in place, using a passive flux and soft solder (see page 43); or if the heat is likely to damage the painted finish, use an epoxy-resin adhesive to attach it. Finally, assemble the components and fold the tab over.

DIE-CAST ZINC

A light gray metal with a low melting point, zinc is used as an alloy with copper to produce brass. Alloyed with small quantities of aluminum and magnesium, it is also the main constituent of die-casting alloys. Although in thin sections zinc castings are relatively lightweight and brittle, it reproduces fine details well and is widely used in the manufacture of model vehicles.

Caring for die-cast toys

The dull gray color of zinc alloy is not particularly attractive, and so it is usually finished with paint. Models are frequently found with chipped or worn paint, but they should not be repainted or touched up, as that can reduce the value to a collector. Place die-cast models in a display cabinet where they are not in contact with one another. Or for long-term storage keep them in their boxes, if they are available. Mint condition models in their original boxes are highly sought after.

Removing dirt
Dust it occasionally with a fine brush to keep the surfaces clean. Wash dirty painted surfaces carefully with cotton wool swabs that are moistened with soapy water (see page 36). Be careful around small projecting details that can bend or break off. If it is necessary, use a small brush. Rinse it with clean water and dry the surface with a soft cloth or absorbent tissue paper.

Making repairs
Small-scale details, such as projecting headlights on models of old cars, are vulnerable to damage. If a part breaks off, reattach it with an epoxy-resin adhesive or instant-setting cyanoacrylate glue. If you are using an epoxy adhesive, brace the part while it sets and use a scalpel to trim away extra adhesive before it has fully set. The joint won't be as strong as the original metal, so handle the repaired model carefully.

CHROMIUM PLATING

Chromium can be recognized easily by its shiny, bright silver color. It is commonly electroplated onto various metals, including brass and zinc castings. In the 1920s it came into vogue as a finish for furniture, lamps, automobile fittings, art objects, and a lot else.

Chromium provides a tough finish that lasts especially well on brass. But poorly applied coatings on steel or zinc alloys may result in the underlying base metal corroding, causing the plating to blister. Little can be done by hand, other than to treat the surface with a proprietary chrome polish. However, since a chrome finish is supposed to have a shiny, bright appearance, it is possible to have items that are in poor condition chemically stripped and replated by a specialist.

IRON AND STEEL

Alloys of iron and carbon form a range of important commercial metals, which are used to produce anything from building structures to industrial and domestic machines, art objects, and utilitarian items of all sizes. The types of metals that are most commonly encountered come under the headings of wrought iron, cast iron, and steel.

Wrought iron is a malleable, low-carbon metal that was once widely used for handcrafted work. A relatively corrosion-resistant iron, it was extensively used for architectural features such as railings, gates, locks, and hinges. Its use declined with the development of cast iron.

Cast iron is a high-carbon metal that has good casting properties. It came into prominence in the nineteenth century, when it was used for the mass production of a wide variety of architectural components and domestic products. It enabled manufacturers to produce highly decorative pieces at a low cost.

Steel is a refined iron alloy that is made in a range of types that vary according to the materials of which it is composed. Plain carbon steel—or "mild steel," as it is generally known—is a common form that can be worked easily by hand in a similar way to traditional wrought iron.

Identifying iron and steel

When iron and steel corrode, they form a red ferrous oxide that is generally known as rust. For protection, both metals are usually finished with paint, oil, or wax, or plated with another metal. In order to establish the nature of the metal under an opaque finish, test it with a magnet: if the magnet sticks, the metal is an iron-based alloy. To identify the type of metal, you need to examine the style and construction of the piece. Wrought iron pieces are typically made from strips or bars that are bent and forged into shape and riveted or welded together. Steel may be used in a similar way. Cast iron pieces may be solid or hollow, depending on their size and shape; since they are made in a mold, molding lines (seams formed where the parts of the mold were connected) are a good indication that an item is cast iron. Another indication of the use of cast iron is a granular surface texture.

Dealing with corrosion

Both iron and steel rust rapidly in damp conditions. After a while, depending on the alloy of the metal, corrosion will produce deep pitting or cause particles to expand and flake off. Keep ironware in a dry place or ensure that the surface is well protected, for example, by microcrystalline wax.

Light rust
To remove light rust, first treat the metal with paraffin for a couple of hours (either leave the piece to soak in the paraffin or brush it onto the surface). Rub off the rust with fine wire pads, then wipe the surface and rinse it with white spirit. Dry the metal and apply a paint finish, lacquer, or microcrystalline wax.

Heavy rust
If a painted surface has failed, it is better to remove the old paint with paint remover before treating the rust. However, if it is important to preserve the paint, try to only clean the rust patches—the edges of the rust probably extend under the finish, so you will need to remove some of the surrounding paint. Scrape the rust with a knife. For large, stripped areas remove loose rust with a wire brush. Apply a commercial rust remover that includes an inhibitor and follow the manufacturer's instructions. To leave a chemically inert surface, wash off the rust remover and dry the iron thoroughly. Protect it with two coats of metal primer and two coats of a compatible top-coat paint.

Sandblasting iron

Sandblasting is an efficient commercial process for removing old paint and rust that leaves the iron with a clean, metallic surface. It is an abrasive process that is not suitable for most domestic ironwork, but it is useful for preparing old cast iron fire grates. Finish the grate with black stove paint, black lead wax, or clear lacquer.

Protecting bright metals

Clean bright metal parts with a spirit solvent such as white spirit or methylene chloride, followed, if required, by a mildly abrasive chrome polish. However, steel is sometimes "blued" (by means of a thin, chemically produced, colored film) as a decorative finish and to inhibit rust—and an abrasive polish should never be used on a blued surface. Depending on the use, protect the cleaned surface with a clear lacquer or microcrystalline wax.

Repairing wrought iron and steel

Wrought iron and mild steel are malleable metals that are likely to bend rather than break. Straighten out bent iron cold in a vice, using leverage or with the aid of a hammer. For thicker sections use a blowtorch to heat the metal first. Be very careful if you have to use heat. If you are in doubt, give the to with a professional. Joints are usually riveted or welded; make simple rivet repairs using iron rivets (see page 42). Welding work can be done by a blacksmith or a local mechanic.

Repairing cast iron

Cast iron is a brittle material and may therefore fracture if it is struck hard or dropped. It is possible to have cast iron welded by a specialist, but for a break that is not structural you can use an epoxy adhesive. Ideally, repair the fracture immediately, in order to ensure that the joint is clean. If it is not, wash the broken edges with a solvent to remove grease and brush off any rust. Try the parts for fit, and then mix the two-part adhesive following the manufacturer's instructions. Apply it sparingly to the broken edges; press the parts together and hold them with clamps or with adhesive tape or a weight. When it has set, trim off any extra glue with a knife.

Repairing mechanical fixings

The individual parts of cast iron products are sometimes held together with machine screws or nuts and bolts. Replace a missing screw with one that matches the thread tht is cut in the metal—this may meean shortening an overlength screw to fit. Hold the waste end in a vice and cut the screw with a hacksaw, then file the end smooth. Similarly, if the originals are rusted or missing, you can fit a new nut and bolt in a bolted joint, where the bolt passes through unthreaded holes in both parts.

IDENTIFYING THE MATERIAL

It is often difficult to identify gemstones and organic materials that are used in jewelry and other artifacts, as all natural materials vary slightly. Identification has been made even more difficult with the use of imitation and synthetic materials. A useful guide is to study the quality of the whole piece. If a piece of jewelry is finely made from precious metals, then it is likely to be of good quality, and the gemstones authentic. Always have old jewelry assessed by a jeweler to establish its value.

Translucent gemstones are usually facet cut and polished to reveal their color and brilliance, whereas semiprecious opaque stones are typically worked into a domed form known as a cabochon. Most of the semiprecious materials that are discussed here are organic in origin and, unlike precious gems, are relatively soft. They are also likely to display a variegated coloring, tend to be larger, and when used for jewelry, they are are usually cabochon cut. Some, such as ivory, shell, and jet, may have decorative tooling.

STORING SEMIPRECIOUS MATERIALS

Treat and store semiprecious jewelry as you would fine-quality pieces. As the material is relatively soft, it is essential each piece is kept in such a way that it cannot be abraded by other, perhaps harder, jewels. Wrap necklaces in acid-free tissue paper. Keep brooches and rings in individual jewel boxes or in a shallow drawer or tray that has separate compartments.

Objets d'art made from these fragile materials should be handled with care. If they are displayed on open shelves, dust them occasionally with a soft cloth or brush to prevent a buildup of dirt. Ideally keep them in dust-free conditions in a glass-fronted display cabinet, which reduces the need to handle them for cleaning and the risk of accidental damage.

For further details see under the individual materials.

SEMIPRECIOUS MATERIALS

People seem to have an innate need to adorn themselves with decorative motifs and materials, as if to compensate for their plainness when they are compared to other creatures. This use of decoration is not restricted to personal adornment, but it also takes the form of applied decoration for functional items and artifacts.

Perhaps it is not surprising that some of these materials are derived from animal as well as vegetable and mineral sources. Tortoiseshell, ivory, bone, seashells, coral, pearl, amber, and jet are just some of the so-called "semiprecious" materials that are used for decorative purposes.

Although their intrinsic value is not as high as that of precious gemstones, they provide a wealth of beautiful materials that can be made into a wonderful range of jewelry and other decorative items. Rare, unusual, and finely crafted pieces are highly sought after by collectors and can command high prices.

It is worth sorting through "junk jewelry" and curios in antique markets, since they often prove to be a source of neglected treasures, which you can restore or use in the repair of other pieces.

JET

Jet is a hard, dense, black variety of lignite, which is a type of coal. It can be worked to a fine, polished finish and was widely used for Victorian mourning jewelry. It was also used for carved decorative pieces that were made for display.

It is sometimes difficult to distinguish jet from black glass imitations, but the real material is somewhat lighter in weight and has a warmer feel. Ebonite—a type of hard rubber, also known as vulcanite—was also used to simulate jet. This can usually be identified by its color, which fades to a rather dull brownish-black. Jet is relatively brittle and chips in a similar way to glass—though the chipped edges tend to have a matt appearance, unlike the shiny chipped surfaces of glass.

Making repairs

Jet is relatively brittle and may break if it is handled roughly. You can repair a clean break using a liquid cyanoacrylate adhesive that is applied sparingly to the broken edges. Test the parts to see if they fit first, since this glue sets instantly. For breaks with ragged edges use a two-part epoxy-adhesive mixed with a black, powdered pigment (available from suppliers of craft materials). This will also act as a filler. When the glue has set, but is not yet fully cured, use a knife to trim off any glue that has exuded from the joint. Once the glue has cured, polish the glue line where the adhesive is acting as a filler, using a mildly abrasive chrome polish. For small holes in a piece that is not subject to wear, you can use a hard, black wax as a filler.

Cleaning jet jewelry

Brush off light dust and wash the jet with cotton buds, cotton wool swabs, or a soft brush that is moistened with a warm solution of liquid dishwashing soap. Rinse it with clean water in the same way and dry with a soft cloth. Do not use solvents, such as white spirit, methylated spirit, or acetone on jet, as these can harm it. Brighten a dulled surface with a mildly abrasive chrome polish. Apply it sparingly, using a cotton bud to polish the surface. Wipe away all traces of the polish and wash it as above.

RESTRINGING A PEARL NECKLACE

Check the thread of a necklace regularly. If it shows signs of wear, replace it before it breaks accidentally. Pearls are strung onto silk thread that is available in a range of sizes and colors, so you should be able to match the original. Some types are supplied with a needle attached—but you can thread the end through the pearls without using a needle, by stiffening the end with a quick-setting adhesive.

1 Arranging the pearls
Cut and remove the old thread, keeping the pearls in their correct order. If they are already loose, arrange them in order of size or color, as required. To hold them in line, fold a length of card-board to make a V-shaped tray.

2 Knotting the thread
Make a half hitch knot around four inches (100mm) from the end. Thread the first pearl up to it and make another knot against the bead. In this way, every pearl is held individually, to avoid losing the whole string of beads if the thread breaks. The knots also prevent the pearls from abrading one another. Use a needle to hold the loop of the knot against the bead as you tighten it. Fasten the remaining pearls in the same way. This method should be used for all good-quality beaded necklaces.

3 Fitting the clasp
Tie off the last pearl, then pass the thread through the clasp ring and back through the pearl. Loop the end around the thread and secure it with a double hitch knot.

4 Finishing the end
Pass the thread through the next pearl and then, while keeping the thread under tension, cut off the surplus thread, flush with the second pearl. The end of the tensioned thread should pull back out of sight into the bead. Attach the other end of the clasp in the same way.

PEARLS

The iridescent white color and natural bead shape of pearls have made them a favorite material for jewelry. They are drilled and strung onto silk thread to make necklaces, or attached to metal mounts to make rings, brooches, and earrings. A natural pearl grows in an oyster over a long period of time and is formed by mother-of-pearl (nacre), which is mainly composed of calcium carbonate, building up on a small speck of grit. Natural pearls tend to be irregular in shape. Cultured pearls are produced by inserting a mother-of-pearl bead into an oyster and leaving it to form layers of nacre in the natural way; this forcing of the process is more likely to result in pearls of a uniform shape. Man-made artificial pearls are molded and colored to look like the real thing, and they can be quite convincing.

Cleaning pearls
The best way to keep pearls in good condition is to wear them. Pearls should not be cleaned with soap and water, since moisture can harm them. Clean them with a dry, light magnesium carbonate powder that is available from drugstores or jewelers. Place the pearls in a sealable container, of a suitable size, almost full of powder. Shake the container for a few minutes, then leave it to stand for around 24 hours. Remove the pearls and clean off the powder with a soft brush and cloth. .

Alternatively, you can use a proprietary cleaning solution that is specially formulated for pearls. Following the manufacturer's instructions, dip the pearl into the container, using the tray provided, and shake it for less than a minute. Lift out the pearls and wipe them dry with a soft cloth.

AMBER

Amber is a natural resin that is exuded by ancient pine trees and fossilized to form a plasticlike material that ranges in color from pale yellow to dark red. The beautiful color of amber and its feel and ease of working with it have been recognized for a long time. It has been used for applied decoration, jewelry and small artefacts since ancient times. Amber pieces sometimes contain seeds or insects that were trapped in the resin when it was still a fluid. Such inclusions add to their value for a collector.

Natural amber is readily polished and displays a variable translucent coloring. This has been successfully imitated in glass and synthetic plastics. Some imitations even include particles, simulating those that are found in the natural resin. A test of authenticity is to heat amber by buffing it with a wool cloth to detect whether it emits a pine-resin aroma. Natural amber also feels warmer than glass.

Ambroid is a reconstituted form of amber. Chips of the natural material are heated and pressed together to form a larger piece. It is not as valuable as fine, selected pieces.

Caring for amber
Amber is relatively soft and fragile, and artifacts that are made from it need careful handling. Keep fine art pieces in a display cabinet and simply dust them occasionally with a soft cloth. Store jewelry in a lined jewelry case and wrap the pieces in acid-free tissue paper for long-term storage. Do not leave amber exposed to strong sunlight, nor in a position where it can be affected by hair spray or perfume atomizers, as these substances can dull the polished surface irreparably.

Cleaning amber
Prolonged exposure to moisture or damp conditions can cause amber to lose its translucency and turn opaque. Although it is possible to clean very dirty amber with warm, soapy water, it must be applied sparingly with cotton buds or swabs and rinsed and dried quickly. Buff the surface with a soft cotton cloth or chamois leather. The application of a little almond oil will help restore the shine. Do not try to clean amber with alcohol or spirit solvents, as these can dissolve and matt the surface.

You can try polishing a matt surface using a mildly abrasive chrome polish, applied with a soft cotton cloth wrapped around your finger. Polish it off with a clean soft cloth.

Making repairs
Although good quality amber pieces should be repaired by a specialist, you can repair a simple break in less significant pieces yourself, using a clear cyanoacrylate adhesive. Apply a very thin film of the glue to the surfaces and press the parts together for an instant bond. Although it is not reversible, it will be less noticeable than an epoxy-resin adhesive, which would be visible through the translucent amber.

A clear, all-purpose adhesive also has the advantage of being invisible, but the amber will be damaged if you have to use a solvent to reverse the bond.

REPAIRING BROOCH FASTENINGS

Brooches are often used for displaying large semiprecious stones, such as amber cabochons. They are usually attached to simple metal mounts for fastening to the garment. These fastenings often fail as a result of wear or rough handling.

Repairing a catch

Catches can be crushed easily and are often broken. Carefully reform a simple bent catch using a pair of needle-nose pliers. Be careful not to overstrain the hook, as the weakened metal can break easily. If the catch is missing, attach a replacement that is made with a flat base, available from a jewelers' supplier.

Grind off the remains of the broken catch, using a miniature power drill and an abrasive wheel.

Bond the catch to the back of the mount, using a two-part epoxy-resin adhesive.

Straightening out a bent pin

The design of the brooch pin will vary according to the quality of the piece. With most pin fastenings, the pin is sprung against a retaining hook. Some also have a locking device.

If the brooch pin is bent, so that it is loose in the catch, reshape it using pliers, working evenly along the pin.

Increasing the tension

The spring tension of the pin is introduced at the hinge end by means of a stop that is formed in the hinge or pin. Adjust the stop or the pin using needle-nose pliers to provide enough spring in the mechanism to hold the pin in the catch.

Replace a broken pin with a new one, which is available from jewelers' suppliers, or have a jeweler make and attach one.

ATTACHING A SAFETY CHAIN

Attach a safety chain as a precaution against losing a valued piece of jewelry. Gold and silver chains are available from jewelers' suppliers. Brooch safety chains have a ring at one end for attaching to the brooch, and a safety pin at the other for fastening onto a garment. Necklace chains have a ring at each end for attaching to the clasp; a bolt ring in the center acts as a secondary clasp and allows the chain to be removed. Bracelet safety chains have a ring at each end for fastening to the clasp.

To attach a chain to the relevant item of jewelry, use needle-nose pliers to open the jump rings (see page 37).

IVORY AND BONE

Ivory is a hard, creamy-white organic material that is versatile as well as attractive. Elephant tusk ivory is the most common type, but hippopotamus and walrus ivory also exist. Ivory is now a protected material, and most countries have imposed an import ban on it. It can be worked with easily, and in the past it was used for large and small figurative carvings, domestic items, jewelry, and decorative veneers and inlays. Bone has similar properties to ivory and is used in a very similar way, although solid pieces are generally smaller.

Ivory and bone can be differentiated by their weight and texture. Ivory is heavier than bone and has a dense, fine grain that polishes well. If you look closely, it is possible to detect concentric growth rings when it is cut transversely. Subtly colored lines or bands that are formed by the layered rings may also be evident over the surface of the piece. Bone has a more porous texture, with dark flecks running along the surface of the polished material.

Old pieces of ivory will naturally mellow to a warm yellow color. Nevertheless, carved pieces were sometimes artificially colored to accentuate the modeling. Old bone tends to be whiter in color.

Although ivory was used as an applied decoration for other materials, ivory pieces were themselves sometimes decoratively engraved, painted, stained, or gilded and were even inlaid with other precious and semiprecious materials.

Caring for ivory and bone

Keep ivory and bone items in stable, moderate conditions, since changes in temperature or humidity can cause the material to expand or contract, which causes distortion or splitting in a similar way to wood. Do not leave pieces close to a window, where direct sunlight or cold or damp conditions can adversely affect the material. Equally, keep pieces away from direct sources of heat, such as radiators or an open fire.

Cleaning

First, remove any dust with a soft brush. Do not use a cloth on inlaid work, as you risk snagging and damaging loose pieces. Wipe the surface of uncolored ivory with a mild solution of warm water and conservator's liquid soap (one part soap to ten parts water), applied sparingly with cotton buds or cotton wool swabs. Rinse it with clean water applied in the same way. Dry the material quickly with a soft cloth to remove any surplus moisture. Do not try to alter the color by using bleach, as you will destroy its antique patina. Finish off with a fine coating of microcrystalline wax to add luster and protect the surface.

Inlays in wood can be dulled by accretions of old wax polish. If the size of the inlay allows for it, carefully clean off the old wax, using white spirit applied with cotton buds. Finish with microcrystalline wax. Where the inlay is too fine to clean with a solvent, just polish the whole surface with microcrystalline wax.

Caring for inlays

Ivory shrinks if it is subjected to overly dry conditions, as will wood. Take good care of inlaid furniture and decorative boxes, as the inlay can work loose and become easily damaged or lost.

Regluing inlays

Reglue loose inlays with PVA adhesive. Work the glue in under the inlay with a brush. Press the inlay into place and wipe all the surplus glue away carefully with a damp cloth. Cover the patch with a piece of polyethylene sheeting and apply a weight to press the inlay down flat. If the inlay has fallen out, carefully scrape out any old glue from the recess, then clean the back of the inlay and glue it back into place.

REPAIRING SILVERWARE

Ivory and bone were popular materials for silverware handles at the turn of the century. Modern versions tend to use simulated handles made out of plastic. Silverware with ivory or bone handles should not be cleaned in a dishwasher, nor left to soak in hot water. Exposure to hot water can cause the handles to distort or loosen.

1 Refitting a handle

The blade of a table knife has a tang that is glued into a hole in the handle, and this can easily work itself loose. Pull the handle off and clean away any old glue from the tang and inside the handle. You may have to devise a wire tool to reach inside the handle or use a suitably shaped needle file or a small gimlet or hand drill.

2 Fixing the handle

Check to see if it fits and apply a two-part epoxy-resin adhesive to the tang and inside the handle. Do not overfill the handle or hydraulic pressure will make it difficult to seat the blade. Push the tang into the handle up to the shoulder. Wipe off any excess glue with methylated spirit, then leave it to set.

TORTOISESHELL

Tortoiseshell is a translucent, organic material that covers the surface of the shells of sea turtles. The most common type comes from the hawksbill turtle. This plasticlike natural material is formed in polygonal plates that make up the domed shape of the shell. When it is heated, it softens and can be pressed flat or molded into other shapes. Heat and pressure also enable it to be connected to create larger sheets.

Tortoiseshell has an attractive mottled coloring that is a mixture of yellow, brown, red, and black. Its transparency also enables colored backgrounds to be used to enhance the coloring. It has been widely used as a decorative veneer for furniture and boxes. The most extravagant examples were introduced by André Charles Boulle (1642-1732), who developed a marquetry technique featuring sheet brass and tortoiseshell that were cut together into ornate floral and geometric patterns. This method produced two sets of perfectly matched inlays—one the reverse of the other. The resulting panel was glued to the surface to produce spectacularly decorative pieces.

Tortoiseshell was also used in veneer or solid form for items such as small boxes, hand mirrors, combs, brush backs, and buttons.

Recognizing the material
Genuine tortoiseshell is no longer available, so treat pieces that are made from it with great care. Modern plastics are now used to reproduce the material and are commonly used for eyeglasses frames. Earlier examples of simulated tortoiseshell were made from celluloid or colored horn. It is not always easy to distinguish between the different materials. Study genuine articles in antique shops to get a "feel" for real tortoiseshell.

Cleaning tortoiseshell
If items include inlay work, remove any dust with a soft brush (not with a cloth), being careful to avoid catching the edge of raised or loose pieces. Clean the surface of tortoiseshell as you would clean ivory, using a minimum amount of warm, soapy water. After drying, if it is lackluster, treat it with almond oil to improve the color. Apply the oil very sparingly and rub it in with a soft cotton cloth wrapped around your finger; repeat if the surface looks patchy and wipe off any surplus. Alternatively, finish off with a thin coating of microcrystalline wax.

If you are fortunate enough to own a fine piece of Boulle work, have it cleaned by a conservator.

Reviving a dull surface
Abrasions or light fogging caused by overexposure to sunlight will leave the surface with a matt finish. Try rubbing them out using a mildly abrasive chrome polish. Apply it with a soft cotton cloth wrapped around your finger, using a circular motion. Wipe off all traces of polish and buff with a soft cloth. Finish off as described above.

Making repairs

Loose pieces of inlaid tortoiseshell are not uncommon, as the animal glue that is used to attach them will weaken over time if it is subjected to moisture or fluctuations in temperature. If they are not already free, carefully remove loose pieces with a fine knife blade. Clean off old glue residues, then reglue (traditionalists prefer to use hot animal glue, but it is easier to use a modern PVA adhesive). Press the inlay into place, then clean off surplus glue, cover it with polyethylene sheeting, and clamp the inlaid surface flat or press it down with weights.

For fractures in solid tortoiseshell pieces, such as a fretted hair slide or a buckle or button, glue the break with clear cyanoacrylate adhesive, applied sparingly.

Missing inlays

Fill in small spaces that are left by missing pieces of inlay with a colored shellac stick used for furniture repairs. Choose a color that has a similar tone to the tortoiseshell. Melt the shellac with an electric soldering iron to fill in the recess. Allow the shellac to set, then carefully shave it flush with a sharp knife or a chisel.

HORN

Horn possesses similar properties to tortoiseshell, and when it is cut into thin, transparent sheets, it is used in much the same way. Like tortoiseshell, horn softens with heat and can be molded into shape. In its natural form it was once used to make powder horns for charging muzzle-loading guns, as well as for domestic items such as combs and handles for walking sticks and umbrellas. Most horn comes from cattle, but horn from other animals is also used. Deer antler, which is more like bone, is commonly used for silverware handles. Maintain horn items in the same way as tortoiseshell.

MOTHER-OF-PEARL

Mother-of-pearl is an iridescent calcium carbonate material—also known as nacre—that forms the inner layer of oyster shells and other similar mollusks. Although it is a relatively hard and brittle material, it cuts well and is often converted into thin sheeting that is used for inlay work, penknife handles, fan sticks, and veneers. Mother-of-pearl can be carved, fretted, and engraved; and it is sometimes dyed to modify its color. It is used for jewelry and decorative items, including dress and shirt buttons, and for domestic items such as silverware handles.

Repairing inlays

Like ivory and tortoiseshell inlay, mother-of-pearl pieces may loosen due to weakened adhesive or to movement in the base material caused by changes in humidity. Because the material is so brittle, do not try to reglue a raised piece that is still partially glued, as there is a risk of breaking it when it is pressed into place. When a piece has fallen out, scrape off any old glue from the back of the inlay and the matching recess. Reglue the inlay with PVA or a clear, all-purpose adhesive.

Cleaning mother-of-pearl

Like pearls, the shell material should not be washed with soap and water. For small objects you can use a pearl dip, which is available from jewelers. Use the dip solution to clean larger pieces or inlay, applying it sparingly with cotton buds or swabs. Rinse it with cotton wool swabs that are dampened with clean, warm water and pat it dry with absorbent tissue.

If accretions of old wax polish have built up in engraved inlays, use toothpicks to scrape away most of the wax, then wipe away the residue with cotton buds that are dampened with white spirit. Be careful not to contaminate the surrounding materials. Revive and protect the cleaned surface with microcrystalline wax.

General repairs

Where items such as jewelry or hair slides have broken in two, glue them together with a cyanoacrylate adhesive if the break is small. If there is a larger gluing area that will not be subject to stress, then you can use a clear, all-purpose adhesive. Reattach silverware handles as described for ivory and bone (see page 59).

CORAL

Coral is a rocklike material that is composed of the calcareous skeletons of tiny marine animals. It forms into beautiful fan and branch shapes that provide the raw material for jewelry and small carvings. Although the most common type is probably red coral (which is actually a pinkish-red), other colors are also found.

Coral is a hard, dense material that polishes to a fine finish. Thin pieces of branch coral are usually drilled and strung onto thread to make necklaces and bracelets or made into brooches, using wire mounts. Other types of corals may be made into beads or cabochons for earrings and brooches.

Cleaning coral
Use cotton buds or swabs that are dampened with a mild solution of liquid dishwashing soap or warm water and conservator's liquid soap (see page 58). Rinse with clean water, then quickly dry the coral with absorbent tissue or a soft cloth. Alternatively, use a proprietary pearl cleaner (see page 55).

Reshaping coral
Red branch coral is often used for earring pendants, complimenting a necklace of a similar design. Pendants tend to be made from larger pieces, and in the case of branch coral they are usually handworked into irregular, tapered shapes.

If an irregular shaped pendant is slightly chipped at the tip, you can remove the mark with abrasive paper, and the shape will help disguise the repair. Tape a sheet of fine wet-and-dry paper to a flat board and lubricate it with water. Rub the coral across it to reform the end into an appealing shape. Apply mildly abrasive chrome polish and buff the reworked surface. If it is necessary, reshape the other pendant to match the reduced size.

Polishing coral
The surface of dull, scratched coral can be polished with a mildly abrasive chrome polish, which is available from auto shops; apply it using a soft cloth or cotton bud, working with a circular motion. Alternatively, to revive the surface of fine pieces, use a miniature power drill with a rubber polishing point coated with polishing compound. Wipe off all surplus polish and buff with a clean, soft cloth.

ORNAMENTAL STONES

Marble, onyx, and alabaster are fine-grained stones that have a gemlike natural beauty when they are cut and polished. Marble—a metamorphic limestone rock—is probably the most common, offering a wide range of mottled and veined colors varying from white to black. It is used for statues, vases, clock cases, bases for ornaments, tabletops, and architectural features such as floor and wall coverings. Onyx is a variety of microcrystalline quartz that has banded markings and is found in various colors, although green is the most popular. It is used for gemstones and for domestic items, including decorative plinths for art deco figurines. Alabaster is an opaque or translucent variety of gypsum that is usually white in color. Its fine texture has been exploited by sculptors for generations, especially in the making of ecclesiastical figurative carvings, but it is also used for domestic items such as clock cases, bases, and vases.

These stones are relatively brittle and porous and mark easily, so handle objects that are made from them carefully. Fine or important works should be treated by professional restorers—but, with care, you can maintain most domestic items yourself.

Caring for ornamental stones

Moisture is the enemy of porous ornamental stones, causing natural salts, frost, mold, and, more critically, acids from atmospheric pollution to attack the surface. If it is possible, they should therefore be kept indoors, in well-ventilated, moisture-free conditions. Because they are porous, they also tend to absorb dirt and stains if they are not protected by a clear wax polish. Acidic substances, including drinks and foodstuffs, etch the polished surface. So quickly clean off any substances that are spilled on them.

Cleaning marble and onyx

Of the two materials, marble is more likely to be encountered in the home, as it was once widely used for mantelpieces and tabletops, urns, and sculptures. The examples of treatment given here refer to marble, but they are also applicable to onyx pieces.

Dust the surfaces regularly with a soft hog hair paintbrush, being careful not to scratch the stone with the metal ferrule that holds the bristles. To be safe, cover the ferrule with adhesive masking tape.

If the surface has become lightly soiled or dowdy, wash it with a solution of conservator's liquid soap and warm water (see page 58), applied with dampened cotton wool swabs. Clean a small area at a time —where applicable, working from the bottom to the top to avoid streaks. Rinse with swabs that are dampened with clean water. Pat dry with a soft, white cotton cloth.

Removing greasy marks

For heavy or greasy soiling, make up a solution of conservator's liquid soap and white spirit. Mix one part soap with ten to twenty parts spirit. This is a powerful degreaser, so wear rubber gloves and protect your eyes against possible splashing. Apply the solution as described above.

Removing light, watersoluble stains

If stains remain after cleaning white marble, try removing them by using a poultice made from shredded white absorbent tissue or an absorbent powder such as whiting. To lift out water-oluble stains, mix the absorbent material with distilled water to form a stiff paste. Apply the poultice in a thick layer over the stain. Leave it in place so that the water can be drawn into the stone in order to activate the stain, which will be absorbed by the poultice as it dries. Wait until the poultice has almost dried, then remove it and rinse the surface of the marble with clean water before drying it off.

Removing oily stains

Prepare a poultice (see opposite) using a solvent, such as lighter fluid, acetone, or clear alcohol, instead of water. Apply a thick coating to the stain and cover it with a patch of polyethylene sheeting, taped in place to prevent rapid evaporation of the solvent. For stubborn stains, you may need to repeat the process. Finally, wash the surface with a liquid soap solution, as used on greasy marks (see opposite).

Bleaching white marble

For persistent unsightly stains in marble work surfaces or tabletops, use 20-volume hydrogen peroxide. Brush this onto the stain and leave it to work, but monitor its progress, then wash the surface thoroughly. Wipe it dry to get a better idea of the result. It may be necessary to repeat the process.

Repairing a chipped edge

Clean the surface thoroughly. Make up a filler of two-part epoxy resin adhesive and white marble or synthetic onyx filler powder, as required. For colored marble, add a small quantity of powdered pigment; you will need to experiment to get the right shade. Overfill the depression and leave the repair to set. Either file the filler to the required contour or sand it with water-lubricated wet-and-dry paper. If need be, wrap the abrasive around shaped wooden blocks. Finish with very fine abrasive paper, then polish it with microcrystalline wax.

Removing scratches

If an otherwise smooth surface is damaged by light abrasions, it is possible to remove them by hand —as long as the remedy will not spoil the piece. Rub out the blemish with very fine flour-grade wet-and-dry abrasive paper, lubricated with water. Where it is possible, work over the surrounding area to avoid creating a local depression. Wash away the slurry and polish the stone with white microcrystalline wax.

Mending broken parts

Make sure that the broken pieces fit well and are clean. Prepare a two-part epoxy resin adhesive and apply a thin film of it to both parts. Clamp them together using rubber bands, adhesive tape, or mechanical clamps, as required. Ensure that the joint is properly aligned. Leave excess glue to set, then trim it flush with a sharp knife. Wash the piece and finish with microcrystalline wax.

MAINTAINING ALABASTER

Alabaster is softer than marble and onyx and can be easily scratched. It is also brittle, so it needs careful handling. Exposure to water will cause the stone to dissolve, so keep it away from damp conditions and from plants that are regularly watered with a sprayer. Do not use water-based cleaning methods on alabaster. For general repairs, follow the methods described for marble.

Cleaning alabaster

Remove dust with a soft brush. To wash the stone, make up a spirit-based cleaner from concentrated liquid soap and white spirit. Mix 1 part soap to 20 parts white spirit. Apply the cleaner with cotton wool swabs, working only a small area at a time. Rinse it with white spirit, applied with clean swabs. Dry it with a soft, white cotton cloth and then polish with microcrystalline wax.

A REASONABLE APPROACH TO RESTORATION

Since china and pottery are inherently fragile, many old pieces are bound to exhibit some form of wear or damage, so don't feel that you have to repair every chip or repaint slightly worn decorations. Although most collectors prefer pieces to be in perfect condition, a degree of damage is often acceptable—and it is certainly preferable to messy or misguided restoration.

Before you decide on a course of action, ask yourself whether the piece will benefit from restoration. Most items look better after they have been cleaned; it also makes sense to repair discolored cracks and to remake badly fitting joints remaining from a previous attempt at restoration.

Items that are in several pieces are obvious candidates, but if you have no previous experience of regluing broken pottery or china, it is advisable to practice first on inexpensive modern crockery. Similarly, if your painting skills are not the best, you can mend and fill the damaged piece but leave retouching until you have mastered the required techniques. The repaired item will look better with obvious but neat fillings than if it is disfigured by thick, inexpertly applied paint.

Always take valuable pieces to a professional restorer for repair, even if the damage or wear is slight.

CERAMICS

Antique china and pottery are highly sought after, both by collectors who acquire them for their aesthetic qualities or for their rarity or financial value, and by people who simply enjoy using or possessing, charming old pieces that cost little to buy yet have a great deal of life left in them.

Ceramics are relatively fragile and therefore prone to damage—indeed it is rare to find old china or pottery in perfect condition. Consequently, it is hardly surprising that many cracked, chipped, and stained pieces are offered for sale at auctions and in antique markets. With a little care and attention, you can restore these items to limited use or add an attractive piece to your collection. Admittedly, restored china does not command the same price as perfect pieces —but then neither do damaged ones.

CLEANING CERAMICS

Most collections, particularly those that are stored on open shelves, benefit from regular dusting and washing. However, the more ceramics are handled, the greater the risk of damaging them. So when you are cleaning your collection, take your time and work methodically to avoid accidents.

Only carry one piece at a time, having removed any separate parts, such as lids, beforehand. Grip each piece firmly, supporting it from below. It is not advisable to rely on the strength of handles or spouts. Never reach to the back of a display shelf to retrieve an item: remove the pieces in front first.

If you have a large collection of ceramics, only clean a small section at a time. This helps maintain concentration and avoids the possibility of too many pieces piling up for washing and drying. Don't wear garments with long, open sleeves when handling or cleaning ceramics—or heavy necklaces, which could swing against a piece of china.

Dusting your collection
It is generally safer to use a soft paintbrush or shaving brush to dust your collection—rather than a cloth or duster, which might become snagged on ornamental details. Before washing ceramics, remove surface dust to prevent dirt from getting washed into cracks and crazing.

Washing ceramics

Washing china simply to freshen up its appearance does not involve prolonged soaking—nevertheless, you should be cautious about immersing repaired ceramics unless you know for certain that the materials used will not be harmed by water. Similarly, obtain expert advice before immersing very old or fragile items. Keep such items clean by dusting them and remove grubby patches with a ball of cotton wool that has been moistened with warm water.

1 Washing by hand
Whatever its condition, never put old china in a dishwasher. Instead, fill a plastic bowl with warm water mixed with a little liquid dishwashing soap. Wash your collection one piece at a time, using an artist's bristle brush to remove dirt from finely-modeled figures or ornaments. Work slowly and deliberately.

2 Rinsing and drying
Rinse each piece individually in clean water, then lay it aside to dry on a tea towel or draining rack. Never stack one piece on top of another. You can dry some pieces with a clean cloth—but blot ornaments and figurines dry with thick paper towel, then if necessary finish the job with a hair dryer that is switched to a relatively cool setting.

Removing stains

Simply washing ceramics in warm water will not remove persistent stains. Dirt or grease that has penetrated into the body of the piece through cracks or fine crazing will need to be drawn out by soaking it in hand-hot water containing biological detergent. The same treatment is required before attempting to assemble broken ceramics, to ensure that the edges of the shards are perfectly clean.

Superficial staining usually disappears after a relatively short period, but you may have to leave stubborn stains to soak for up to a couple of weeks, changing the hot detergent solution from occasionally.

In all probability, prolonged soaking will begin to break down old repairs (see page 70)—so, before soaking, examine each piece carefully for signs of retouching and glued joints.

1 Immersing in hot water
Fill a plastic bowl or bucket with a solution of detergent in hot water. Immerse the stained item or broken pieces and leave them to soak for at least 20 minutes, swirling the water gently and scrubbing dirty cracks and broken edges with an old toothbrush.

2 Rinsing in clean water
As soon as you are satisfied with the result, rinse each item in clean cold water—fill the bowl to overflowing and leave the faucet running for around five minutes.

3 Drying the piece
Dry the pieces by hand with a soft cloth, then put them in an oven, heated to 220°F, for about half an hour. At this point some items will exude still more grease from deep inside the ceramic body, in which case repeat the soaking and drying process.

Bleaching stains

For speed, many restorers resort to bleaching stained ceramics, rather than leaving them to soak. However, bleach can cause a stain to spread, particularly through absorbent pottery. Also, if you fail to rinse all the bleach out of the ceramic body, then it may eventually cause problems with painted-over repairs. However, as long as retouching with paint or glaze is not required, bleaching is a viable option for cleaning hairline cracks in porcelain or stoneware prior to gluing. Seek professional advice before bleaching anything made earlier than the nineteenth century, and be very careful with gilded pieces.

1 Preparing bleach
Wearing protective vinyl gloves, pour some 100-volume hydrogen peroxide into a saucer and dilute it with three parts water, then add a few drops of household ammonia. The fumes are not pleasant, so work in a well-ventilated area and wear a face mask.

2 Applying bleach
Soak the piece in clean water, then use tweezers to dip cotton wool swabs into the bleach solution and apply them to the hairline crack.

3 Leaving the bleach to work
Seal the piece in a plastic bag to keep the swabs moist. Keep an eye on its progress for around two hours, then if necessary apply fresh swabs and reseal the bag. When the crack is clean, rinse the piece thoroughly in clean water.

DISMANTLING OLD REPAIRS

Restorers are often faced with the problem of having to dismantle previous restorations, either to replace old, discolored glue with a stronger modern adhesive or simply to improve an unsatisfactory repair.

Soaking in hot water
In most cases you can break down old glue by leaving the piece to soak in hot water containing biological detergent (see page 69)—this has the advantage of cleaning the item thoroughly at the same time.

1 Easing the joints apart
After around 20 minutes the hot water will begin to soften the majority of glues. Try easing the joints apart, but don't flex them, or you may chip the fragile edges. Be careful at this stage, because hot, soapy water makes china slippery, and it is all too easy to cut yourself on the sharp shards.

2 Using the point of a knife
Once a joint begins to separate, you can insert the point of a knife blade to prize the two pieces apart. Scrub the residue of glue from the edges with an old toothbrush, picking off any remaining specks of glue with the knife. Dry the shards in an oven (see page 69).

Using paint stripper
No amount of soaking will soften some modern glues, so your only recourse may be to apply a proprietary water-based paint stripper. Examine the piece beforehand to make sure that there is no surface decoration that could be harmed by the stripper—and if necessary, apply the stripper to the undecorated side of the piece only. Wear protective gloves and follow the manufacturer's recommendations.

Having attempted to resolve the problem by soaking the piece in hot water, simply rinse the piece in cold water and apply the stripper. If you have allowed the item to dry, soak it again in clean water before proceeding.

1 Applying paint stripper
Paint a gel, all-purpose stripper along each glued joint. Alternatively, dip balls of cotton wool in a liquid stripper and place them side by side along the joints. After 20 minutes scrape the stripper from the surface and check for signs of movement. If need be, apply fresh stripper.

2 Washing off the stripper
Prize the joints apart, as described on the left, then transfer the pieces to a bowl of hot water and add some biological detergent. Wearing eye protection in case of splashes, scrub and rinse the pieces thoroughly to remove softened glue and stripper (see page 69).

Removing rivets

Before the development of reliable adhesives, damaged pieces were sometimes stapled together with metal "rivets." As long as the joints are still sound, there is little point in removing rivets unless you find them especially unattractive. However, if the piece requires additional restoration or is beginning to come apart, your best course of action is to remove the rivets and apply a modern epoxy resin glue.

EXAMPLES OF EARLIER RESTORATION SHOWS THE USEOF RIVETS AND DISCOLORED GLUE LINES

1 Picking the plaster out
The folded end of each rivet is located in a hole that has been drilled in the ceramic body and embedded in plaster. Soften the plaster by soaking the piece in hand-hot water, then pick the plaster out with a pointed tool and pull out each rivet with pliers.

2 Removing stubborn rivets
Occasionally it is impossible to remove a rivet until you cut it in half, using a miniature power tool with a cutting disk.

Alternatively, a rivet may be embedded in lead solder, in which case place the tip of a soldering iron onto the rivet until the solder melts, then pull the rivet out immediately.

DEALING WITH RIVET STAINS

If they are subjected to damp or humid conditions, metal rivets can corrode and stain the ceramic body with oxides.

Neutralizing rust stains
To remove rust marks that surround old rivets, use phosphoric acid that is sold in gel form for treating rusty cars. Wearing protective gloves, apply the gel to the stains and leave it in place for 15 to 20 minutes. Wipe the gel from the surface and, if necessary, make further applications until the stain has been reduced to an acceptable level. Finally, wash the area with water and dry it thoroughly with a hair dryer.

Swabs of cotton wool soaked in acetone or cellulose thinners may remove copper stains.

MENDING BROKEN CERAMICS

Every ceramics restorer must develop the ability to make accurate glued joints, as no amount of filling or repainting will disguise inept work. Edges that are to be joined must be perfectly clean, since even the tiniest speck of dried glue can make it impossible to bring the surfaces together tightly.

PVA ADHESIVE

CYANOACRYLATE GLUE

TITANIUM DIOXIDE

EPOXY RESIN GLUE

GLUES FOR CERAMIC RESTORATION

There are a number of adhesives that are recommended by professional restorers, but the most useful one for amateurs is two-part epoxy resin glue, which can be bought from any hardware store. When the two components are mixed in equal proportions, the glue begins to set by chemical reaction, forming an extremely strong, waterproof joint. Epoxy resin glue is practically transparent, but if there is the slightest risk of a perceptible glue line on white-bodied ceramics, add a pinch of titanium dioxide (a white powder that is available from craft materials suppliers) to the mixed glue. Conventional epoxy resin glue sets hard within a few hours, but it continues to gain strength over time, especially if the repaired piece is warmed in an oven.

Epoxy resin glues are suitable for use with all types of ceramics, but some restorers prefer to use a water-based PVA woodworking adhesive to repair porous earthenware. In order to ensure a strong joint, the edge of each shard must be moistened with water before the glue is applied.

If it is necessary, a PVA adhesive is reversible by immersion in water. Theoretically, epoxy resin glues are irreversible, but in practice they can be softened with paint stripper (see page 70).

Cyanoacrylates (superglues) are marketed as general-purpose glues. Although they are rarely recommended by professionals for antique restorations, they do have their uses—especially for tacking together a complicated assembly (see opposite).

Repairing a crack

A hairline crack is worth gluing, not only to improve the appearance of a piece but also to prevent the crack from extending farther. Make sure that the crack is clean by washing the item in a solution of biological detergent (see page 69) or by bleaching it with hydrogen peroxide.

1 Introducing glue
Warm the damaged piece for five minutes in an oven heated to 220°F. Wearing oven mitts, transfer the piece to your workbench and use a toothpick to run epoxy resin glue sparingly along the crack. The heated ceramic will liquidize the glue and draw it into the crack. If the ceramic body is relatively thick, insert a razor blade to open up the crack slightly before introducing the glue from both sides.

2 Strapping the crack together
Remove the razor blade and wipe any excess adhesive from the surface, using a cloth that has been moistened with methylated spirit, then stretch one or two strips of adhesive tape across the crack. Put the piece back into the oven for ten minutes to help the glue cure. Let the piece cool down, then remove the tape and pare the residue of adhesive from the surface with a sharp knife.

Assembling broken china and pottery

Gather together all the fragments of the broken item and wash them thoroughly, then dry them in an oven for 30 minutes (see page 69).

Before you mix the glue, make a "dry run," taping the joints together to make sure that you have all the pieces—and also, by rehearsing the procedure, to check that every fragment can be inserted without having to dismantle part of the assembly, and none of them is "locked out."

1 Begin with one of the larger fragments

Begin by sticking strips of adhesive tape to both sides of one of the larger fragments, so that the strips overhang the broken edge by half their length.

2 Applying adhesive

Use a toothpick to apply epoxy resin glue sparingly to the edge of the next fragment. Press both pieces together, rocking them slightly to exclude as much glue as possible and to encourage the edges to match up perfectly. Fold back each strip to prevent it from getting in the way.

3 Strapping the joint together

Holding the pieces together firmly, stretch each piece of tape across the joint. Wipe off any excess adhesive and check the accuracy of the assembly by rubbing your thumbnail across the joint. If you can feel the slightest misalignment, slacken one or more strips of tape, adjust the fit, and stretch the tape back into place.

4 Completing the assembly

Continue gluing one fragment to the next, following the sequence derived from your "dry run." When the assembly is complete, put it in the oven for ten minutes. Once the ceramic is cool enough to touch, peel off the adhesive tape and pare off any dried glue adhering to the surface.

Tacking together a complicated assembly

Strapping each joint with adhesive tape can be impossible when you have to assemble many small fragments. Instead, tack the fragments together, using tiny spots of cyanoacrylate glue, which sets in seconds. Work meticulously to ensure that each joint is perfect, dissolving the glue with acetone or cellulose thinners if you have to start again.

The completed assembly will be fragile, but it should be strong enough to place in an oven, heated to 220°F, for around five minutes. As soon as you take the assembly out of the oven, run epoxy glue into each joint, the same as for repairing a hairline crack (see opposite). At this stage the job may look unsightly. Put the assembly back in the oven for ten minutes, and the glue should then be hard enough for you to scrape the surface clean, once it is cool enough to touch.

DEALING WITH WARPED PIECES

When china or pottery breaks, tensions are released that sometimes cause one or more fragments to warp. This makes it impossible to align them in the conventional way.

One possible solution is to apply epoxy resin glue to both meeting edges, only halfway along their length. Strap the relevant section firmly together with tape, then carefully pull the unglued edges together with more tape.

When the glue has set hard, remove the tape from the unglued section, introduce glue into the gap, and tape the joint securely.

FILLING JOINTS

It is very rare for a ceramic piece to have a clean break. If you examine the fragments closely, you will invariably find that their edges are chipped and, in order to make a perfect repair, that it will require filling after they have been glued.

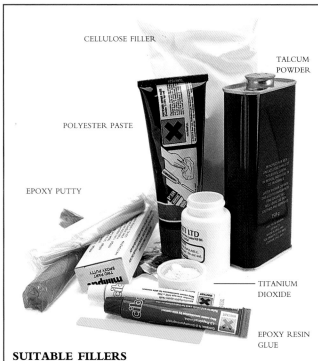

CELLULOSE FILLER

TALCUM POWDER

POLYESTER PASTE

EPOXY PUTTY

TITANIUM DIOXIDE

EPOXY RESIN GLUE

SUITABLE FILLERS

You can buy fine ready-made surface fillers and putties that are ideal for repairing ceramics, or you can make your own using epoxy resin glue as a base.

White two-part epoxy putty—which is available from many hardware stores and modeling stores—begins to set as soon as the constituents are kneaded together. To make your own epoxy putty, mix titanium dioxide and talcum powder with two-part epoxy resin glue.

Polyester paste—manufactured for patching rusty car bodies—also works as an excellent filler for ceramics: a red hardener mixed with the thick, gray paste produces a pink filler, but you can modify the color by adding a pinch of titanium dioxide.

These fillers can be used to repair a variety of ceramics, ranging from hard-paste porcelain to earthenware. For porous earthenware, however, many restorers prefer to use decorator's cellulose filler (either buy a tub of ready-made paste or mix a powdered filler with water).

1 Inserting filler
Use a dental spatula or the tip of a knife blade to press the filler into the minute holes and crevices, spreading it across each joint from different angles. Then run the blade or spatula along the joint to scrape the filler flush with the piece.

2 Removing excess filler
To smooth out epoxy paste, moisten your fingertip and wipe it lightly along each joint—having to refill later is preferable to sanding down lumps of hardened filler.

3 Sanding down
Allow the filler to harden thoroughly, then sand along all the joints with extra-fine (400 to 600 grade) wet-and-dry paper. To protect overglaze decoration from damage, restrict the sanding to as small an area as possible by cutting the paper into two inch (50mm) squares and folding them into narrow strips.

Repairing chipped edges

The vulnerable rims of earthenware and china often exhibit small "shell" chips, especially decorative plates that have been hung from wire plate hangers. Fortunately this type of damage is easy to repair, using any of the putties or pastes recommended for filling glued joints.

Scrub the chipped edges with hot water containing biological detergent (see page 69). To help epoxy putty adhere, paint epoxy resin glue thinly onto the surface of the chip right before you fill it.

1 Applying filler
Press the filler into place, smoothing it into shape with a modeling tool or a moist fingertip.

2 Sanding it flush
Once the filler has hardened, shape the repair with a fine file and smooth it with wet-and-dry paper.

USING DENTAL WAX

As an alternative to modeling clay, you can use strips of dental wax (available from specialist craft suppliers) to make a simple press molding (see top right). Smear petroleum jelly onto the area from which you intend to take the impression, then soften a strip of dental wax over a source of heat and press it into place. You may have to apply a second strip over the first to make the mold thick enough to retain its shape. Reposition the mold and fill it in as described (right).

Molding a broken rim

If part of a rim has broken off, take an impression from an intact section of the rim and use it as a mold for reproducing the missing part. If the item is made with raised decorations, be sure to take the impression from the molded side of the rim.

It is difficult to ensure a good bond to a very narrow broken edge. As a precaution, complete the filling but, before you sand it smooth, knock it out and glue it back into place with epoxy resin glue, then fill in the joint.

1 Taking the impression
Use a cotton wool swab to moisten the area from which you intend to take an impression, then press a slab of children's modeling clay ½ inch (12mm) thick against the rim.

2 Repositioning the mold
Gently prize the clay off the mold, being careful not to distort its shape, and locate it over the damaged section of the rim. To hold it in place, carefully fold the clay over the rim at each end of the mold.

3 Filling in the mold
Dust the clay mold with talcum powder to act as a release agent and gently press epoxy putty or polyester paste into the mold. Be careful to cover the inner face of the mold before building up the thickness of the damaged section—if need be, let the first layer harden before you attempt to fill it in flush.

4 Smoothing the repair
Try to copy the contours of the piece as closely as possible, shaping the filler with a moistened filling knife. Leave the filler to harden overnight, then peel off the mold and smooth the repair with wet-and-dry paper. If one side of the repair includes raised decorations, you may have to remodel some of the fine details, using epoxy putty.

REPAINTING REPAIRED CERAMICS

Retouching damaged patterns and matching the background color and glaze are the most difficult aspects of ceramics restoration. There are no shortcuts: only practice and a good eye for color will eventually produce successful results. However, it makes the work easier if you are able to buy the best-quality materials and equipment—especially if your budget can cover an airbrush that enables you to spray over filled repairs, leaving an indiscernible edge to the paint.

STOVE-ENAMELING GLAZE

GLAZE THINNERS

ACRYLIC VARNISH

AIRBRUSH

SABLE BRUSHES

OIL PAINTS

ACRYLIC PAINT

Materials and equipment

You will need two or three artist's paintbrushes. Choose good-quality sable brushes that come to a fine point every time they are used.

An airbrush is a finely adjustable spray gun that is operated by compressed air, which is supplied in aerosol cans or by means of an electrically-powered compressor. Cans of compressed air are cheaper to begin with, but a compressor will eventually pay for itself if you specialize in ceramic restorations.

Use artist's acrylic paints to match the background color of the piece that you are working on and a similar acrylic varnish to simulate the original glaze. Both the paints and the varnish can be thinned with water.

Alternatively, follow the example of professional restorers, who use a low-firing, stove-enameling glaze that is specially formulated for ceramics. This type of glaze sets after being heated in an ordinary domestic oven. Most professionals prefer an electric stove that maintains an accurate temperature, but you can use a gas oven or a solid-fuel stove. To color the background, add artist's oil paints to the clear stove-enameling glaze and dilute it with cellulose thinners or the special thinner that is sold with the glaze. Don't be tempted to economize by buying cheap oil paints—they are likely to discolor after being heated in an oven.

If you are using an airbrush, it is essential that you work in a well-ventilated workshop that is equipped with an efficient extractor fan. You should also wear a respirator. Whatever equipment you use, illuminate your workbench with a simulated-daylight lightbulb to ensure that your color matching is accurate.

Painting by hand

Restoring paint and glaze by hand—using paintbrushes to apply the color and transparent varnish—has the advantage of being relatively inexpensive and offers a measure of control that is appealing to novice restorers. However, the second of these advantages is somewhat illusory, as full control of any medium is rarely easy.

The techniques described here all involve using air-drying acrylic paints and varnishes—but it is also possible to apply stove-enameling glaze by hand.

Matching the background color

Mixing colors perfectly is a process of trial and error that is guided by experience. Even a so-called white background is always biased toward the "warm" or "cool" end of the spectrum. Adding a speck of brown or yellow to white paint warms the color up slightly, while blues or greens cool it down.

1 Mixing and testing the color

In practice, the best way to match the color of the background is to use a white tile or a saucer as a palette for mixing the paints, then brush a small dot of the mixed color onto the body of the ceramic itself. Wipe it off immediately with a paper towel and continue to adjust the color balance until you are satisfied with the match.

2 Applying the paint

Brush the paint smoothly onto the filled area, working from the center of the repair toward the edges. You should avoid applying the paint too thick, but it needs to flow out naturally and cover the filler without having to make a second application. Tentative brushstrokes tend to show as permanent marks in the paint as it dries.

3 Feathering the edges

The aim is to cover the filled areas only, with the paint spreading as little as possible onto the undamaged surfaces of the ceramic piece. As you approach the perimeter of the repair, wash your brush and squeeze it dry, leaving the tip of the brush fan-shaped. Using very light strokes, drag the edge of the paint out onto the glazed surface until it is feathered out to nothing. Leave the paint to dry in a dust-free environment.

4 Rubbing it down

If the new paint dries to a slightly different color or the surface is less than perfect, rub it down lightly with very fine self-lubricating silicon-carbide paper—a gray abrasive that is dusted with fine white powder available from hardware stores and modeling stores. After rubbing it down, apply a second feathered coat of paint.

Recreating missing patterns

Once you are satisfied with your base color, you can touch up any missing patterns or surface coloring. Use the remaining pattern as a guide for color and shape and apply the paint as described (left), feathering off the edges of the new paint as much as possible. If you make a mistake or cover too much of the original paint correct it immediately with the tip of a clean brush or a toothpick that is moistened with water.

Applying clear varnish

When the colored paint is dry, flow on a coat of clear acrylic varnish and feather the edges as you did for the base color. It is very important to protect the setting varnish from airborne dust—but if it is necessary, you can leave it to harden, then rub it down and apply a second coat.

USING AN AIRBRUSH

A single-action airbrush has a button that releases the flow of air, while a separate control (usually mounted at the rear end of the handle) regulates the amount of paint or varnish that is delivered to the nozzle. This type of airbrush is relatively easy to use —having set the fluid control, you can concentrate on placing the paint exactly where you want it.

On a double-action airbrush the air supply and spray pattern are controlled by a single trigger. In the hands of an experienced artist the double-action airbrush is more versatile, but it is difficult to master initially. Whichever type of airbrush you decide to buy, check with your supplier that it has a fluid tip and needle that are capable of spraying relatively thick finishes.

Since the average restoration requires very little paint or varnish, an airbrush that has a small side cup or paint reservoir is convenient.

The various techniques that are described here use stove-enameling glaze mixed with oil paints.

Controlling an airbrush
Hold the airbrush as if you were using a pen or pencil, in a relaxed grip with the first joint of your index finger resting on the control button. Drape the air hose over your wrist.

1 Mixing the paint
It is convenient to mix the glaze in the airbrush reservoir, then to paint spots of color onto the ceramic piece with a fine brush to see if you have achieved an accurate match (see page 77). Mix 50 percent glaze and thinners, then gradually add the colored oil paint as required.

2 Covering the filler
Because an airbrush applies very thin coats of glaze, begin by spraying the repaired areas with pure white glaze to highlight any blemishes that may require further filling and rubbing down.
*   Holding the tip of the airbrush close to the piece, spray a narrow line of glaze along each filled joint. Take a clean paintbrush that is moistened with thinner and carefully wipe away any excess glaze.*

3 Adding background color
Put the sprayed piece in an oven, heated to 220°F, for around 45 minutes, then remove it and leave the ceramic piece to cool down. Spray over the repairs again, this time with a glaze that is matched to the background color. Return the piece to the oven for a further 45 minutes.

4 Adding patterns
Either use the airbrush to spray in areas of graduated color or mix oil paint to the glaze and copy hard-edge patterns by hand, using a paintbrush. Heat the painted piece in the oven for another 45 minutes.

5 Spraying with clear glaze
Finally, spray over the restored paint with a coat of clear glaze. To simulate a matt glaze, add a pinch of fumed silica (a very fine white powder that is available from drugstores) to the stove-enameling glaze. It is essential that you heat the final coat of glaze for a full hour.

SPECIAL EFFECTS

However skillful the repair may be, areas of freshly applied paint are sometimes a little too "clean" to merge unobtrusively with old ceramic glazes and finishes. The solution may be to tint the final coat of clear glaze with the slightest bit of oil paint to give it a suitably aged appearance. Occasionally it takes a little more to fool the eye.

Reproducing a crazed finish
The glaze on many old pieces of china and pottery is crazed, either deliberately during the manufacturing process or through shrinkage. Copy the pattern of cracks onto the body color before you apply a coat of clear protective glaze. This requires a steady hand and either a very sharp colored pencil or the finest brush and thinned paint or glaze.

Recreating unusual glazes
Metallic luster glazes are notoriously difficult to replicate, and it is sometimes easier to settle for the effect of an old rubbed glaze rather than attempt to make a perfect finish. This is achieved by spraying the repair with the background color of the original luster glaze (say dark brown or gray) and then, when it is dry, spraying over it with a clear glaze containing a suitable blend of metallic powders (see right).

A similar technique is useful when you need to repair a dark-bodied ceramic piece that is finished with a translucent white glaze. First cover the filler with the dark color, then apply a coat of thin white glaze that allows the background color to show through.

REPAIRING GILDING

Many antique pieces are decorated with gold paint or, in some cases, with real gold leaf. Gold leaf tends to only be used on old and valuable items, and it invariably pays to have these restored by an expert. Average collectables can be retouched with gilt varnish, which is available from craft suppliers or by mail order. You can also buy gilt and bronze powders in various shades for mixing with turpentine or thinned stove-enameling glaze.

Gilding a rim
Antique bowls, cups, and saucers are often finished with gilt rims that have to be retouched after a repair. Instead of trying to paint a straight line in the conventional manner, rest your painting arm on a support, such as a thick book, and revolve the piece around the tip of the brush.

USING AND DISPLAYING CHINA

Unless it is stored in extreme conditions, antique china does not get damaged easily from the effects of moisture or dust. Airborne pollution can cause exposed paint to turn black, but this can be fixed easily by rubbing it very gently with a plastic scouring pad and water.

The majority of repaired items are only suitable for display cabinets. Heat or frequent washing is likely to discolor retouched repairs and may break down glued joints. Reglued handles are particularly vulnerable.

Even when old china is basically sound, check to see if the glaze has crazed—since fats from foodstuffs and sauces can penetrate and stain the ceramic body. Always wash and sterilize old ceramic items before using them for serving food, but don't be tempted to put them in a dishwasher.

Glass-fronted cabinets

The best way to display antique ceramics is probably in a glass-fronted cabinet. The pieces are kept relatively dust free, and they are safe from prying hands. Whether the cabinet is modern in style or a period piece to match the china is a matter of personal taste, but the latter can be bought very reasonably. Glass shelves are generally an advantage since they allow more light to be reflected into the cabinet. Artificial lighting built within the cabinet itself is also an attractive option. Check that a cabinet is standing solidly —walking across a suspended wooden floor may be enough to start your collection rattling, with unfortunate consequences.

Veneered display cabinet in the art deco style

Open shelves

On open shelves, which may be the only realistic option for a sizable collection, china can be exhibited attractively and without distracting reflections caused by glass doors. However, you have to be prepared to dust on a regular basis. Choose or make shelves with a longitudinal groove to hold the rims of the plates standing on edge. Alternatively, attach a narrow strip of wood to the shelf.

Plate stands and hangers

To display individual plates or cups and saucers, buy stands that are built out of plastic-covered metal rods or molded plastic. Sprung-wire plate hangers are perfect for displaying china on a wall where you cannot install a cabinet or shelving. However, plate hangers can damage ceramics if they are carelessly applied. To prevent chipped rims, locate the wire hooks carefully and slip thin cardboard packing between the back of the plate and the hanger's coil springs to stop them from rubbing against the base.

Old dressers are ideal for exhibiting ceramics collections

Display plates to utilize inaccessible wall space

A DURABLE MATERIAL

Although it is brittle, glass is a strong, durable material that is unaffected by atmospheric changes, except for extreme conditions of moisture, light, or heat. As a result, the glassware that has come down to us is often in excellent condition. If it has survived at all, it rarely needs very much restoration.

Another reason for the scarcity of restored glassware is that there is only so much that successfully can be done to repair glass, even by experts. Other than craftsmen and craftswomen who restore stained glass and leaded lights, there are relatively few practicing professionals who specialize in glass restoration. If you have very old and valuable pieces that are in need of care or repair, it is therefore probably the best solution to seek out a ceramics restorer who is also experienced at mending glassware.

GLASS COLLECTABLES

Nowadays glass is such a common and inexpensive material that we tend to take it for granted—but, because of its beauty and versatility, it has been used for thousands of years to make a staggering range of decorative and utilitarian objects.

Glass is made by fusing silica in the form of sand, flint, or quartz with a flux, such as potash, soda, or lead, at a high temperature. Adding various oxides to the mix produces colored glass.

While it is molten, glass can be extruded, blown, molded, or rolled to create a seemingly endless variety of shapes. And when it has cooled down, it is frequently embellished by cutting, etching, engraving, sandblasting, painting, or gilding.

CLEANING GLASS

Except for fragile old glass that has been buried—possibly even for centuries—you can generally wash glassware in water without any fear of harm.

However, examine painted pieces to make sure that the decoration is waterproof and not about to flake off; and don't immerse glass bottles and other containers that still have their original paper labels attached. Similarly, don't soak glassware that exhibits signs of previous restoration, in case the glue or paint that was used is not waterproof.

Wash antique glassware by hand—never in a dishwasher—and dust each piece before washing it, using a soft bristle paintbrush.

2 Soaking glassware
Leave very dirty pieces to soak for a couple of hours. Some glassware can be difficult to see in the water, so lay a tea towel across the bowl and leave a note beside it to warn others that there is glass soaking inside.

1 Washing by hand
Fill a plastic bowl with hand-hot water containing biological detergent. To avoid knocking glassware against the faucet, place the bowl on a draining board or work surface rather than in your kitchen sink.

Wash each piece individually, cleaning it with a piece of soft cloth, and use a paintbrush to remove the dirt from engravings or finely cut decorations. When you are washing old glass bottles, you will probably need a specialized bottle brush to scrub the insides clean.

3 Rinsing in tepid water
Rinse the glassware in a bowl of clean tepid water. A few drops of methylated spirit added to the water will give the glass a nice sparkle.

4 Drying glassware
Dry each piece carefully with a soft tea towel—don't polish drinking glasses with a twisting action, because you are liable to snap pieces of glass. Instead, wipe straight from the bottom of the bowl toward the rim.

Drying decanters

It is important to ensure that moisture does not become trapped inside a stoppered decanter because it could turn the glass cloudy. Having dried the outside with a tea towel, leave the decanter upside down in a plastic bucket to dry naturally. Dry the stopper separately.

Removing stains

As a rule, glass is affected by two types of staining—the white cloudiness that is associated with moisture and hard water lime scale and the stains that are left by the contents (typically red wine).

To remove white water staining, try leaving the stain soaking overnight in denture cleaner, then rinse and dry the piece thoroughly.

Cover a red-wine stain with clear "white" vinegar and leave it for 24 hours, then wash, rinse, and dry the glassware.

If the glass has become etched, neither treatment will have the desired result.

Washing perfume bottles

Although many collectors keep antique perfume bottles solely for display, others like to use glamorous-looking bottles for their original purpose. Before you refill an old bottle, remove the smell of stale perfume by filling the bottle with methylated spirit and leaving it to soak for around an hour.

Keep refilling it with fresh spirit until the stale smell disappears, then wash the bottle out in warm, soapy water and rinse it thoroughly. Dry perfume bottles carefully—if need be, by drying the inside with a hair dryer on a cool setting.

Swabbing glassware

To wash glass that cannot be immersed in water, wipe the surface clean with swabs of cotton wool that are dipped in a warm solution of biological detergent. Wash a large item from the bottom upward, to avoid leaving dirty streaks on the glass. Swab the piece with cold water, then dry it with a clean tea towel. Finally, polish it with methylated spirit on a cloth to make the glass sparkle.

Washing glass lusters

Often, chandeliers are constructed from small glass droplets known, as lusters, that reflect the light in all directions. When they become covered with greasy deposits, nicotine, or dust, lusters lose their sparkle and require washing. Although it is generally advisable to have a large chandelier cleaned by an expert, you may want to clean candlesticks or oil lamps with lusters yourself.

If you are able to dismantle the piece, you can wash individual lusters in a bowl of warm, soapy water—but either remove the metal links before you immerse the lusters or make sure that you dry the metal thoroughly to avoid rusting.

Alternatively, swab the lusters as described (below left) and polish them with a rag that is moistened with spirit.

Cleaning enamel

Enamel is a form of colored glass that is fused to a metal base. Among its many applications, enamel is used to make highly decorative jewelry, buttons, and small boxes. Chipped or cracked enamel can allow moisture to penetrate, causing the metal backing to corrode and the enamel to flake off. Consequently, it is best to clean enameled collectables by dusting with a soft paintbrush and removing greasy deposits with cotton wool that is barely moistened with acetone.

REPAIRING GLASS

As a rule, once a piece of glassware is cracked or broken, it can never safely be used for its original purpose. However, aside from the desire to preserve a piece of antique glassware, it is a good idea to stabilize cracked glass or glue a shard back into place as soon as possible to prevent an accident.

Don't attempt to restore valuable glass yourself; wrap it up carefully and take it to a conservator.

SUITABLE ADHESIVES

Since most glass is transparent, it is difficult to make an invisible glued repair. A restorer usually has to settle for a neat repair that allows the object to be displayed in a showcase, even though it will not stand up to close scrutiny. It is somewhat easier to make a discreet repair with opaque or dark-colored glassware—but because it is difficult to fill in repairs satisfactorily, you are still left with a glue line that is fairly obvious with close inspection.

Don't allow glue to spread onto the surface of etched or sandblasted glass, in case it dries as a shiny patch.

Be careful when you are gluing shards of glass together—they are extremely sharp.

Ultraviolet-curing adhesive

Clear, glass-bonding adhesive is available from any good hardware store. When it is exposed to the ultraviolet rays that are present in natural daylight, the adhesive begins to cure rapidly, setting within ten seconds in bright sunlight and after around two minutes on a cloudy day.

Since artificial tungsten light doesn't affect the adhesive, the most efficient method is to work under artificial light at a table in front of a window with the curtains drawn; then once you have achieved an accurate glued joint, open the curtains to expose the adhesive to daylight.

Epoxy resin adhesive

Ultraviolet-curing glue is not suitable for repairing opaque or dark-colored glass. Instead, use a two-part epoxy resin adhesive (see page 72). Before you mix the adhesive, warm the two tubes on a radiator to make the glue less viscous. Alternatively, it is possible to use a clear liquid epoxy resin adhesive, though it is not as readily available.

All-purpose adhesive

Although the repair will not be as strong as with the other recommended glues, you can stick broken glass together with a clear all-purpose adhesive (this is not a cyanoacrylate glue).

Mending cracked glass

Cracked glass is only obvious because the air that is trapped inside the crack stands out as a silvery streak. If you can exclude the air, the crack is hardly noticeable.

Run a narrow bead of ultraviolet-curing adhesive along a crack, then blow the glue into the crack to disperse the air. Wipe any excess glue from the surface of the glass, using a cloth that is moistened with acetone.

Cure the adhesive by exposing it to daylight, then pare hardened glue off the surface by running a knife blade along the crack.

Reassembling broken glass

Before gluing a shard of glass back into place, clean the broken edges extremely carefully, using a cotton wool bud that is dampened with acetone.

1 Applying adhesive

Check that there are no strands of cotton wool adhering to the glass, then apply ultraviolet-curing adhesive sparingly to one broken edge. Bring both pieces together, rocking them gently to exclude any excess glue and to ensure that the edges match up perfectly. Strap the repair with clear adhesive tape and, if necessary, exclude air from the joint as described for mending cracked glass (see above).

2 Cleaning up
Expose the glue to daylight. When the glue has set hard, pare any residue off the surface with a sharp knife and remove any smears with acetone.

3 Filling in small chips
Since glass rarely makes a clean break, you can usually detect small holes along the joint where tiny pieces of glass were chipped off the broken edges. Although it is impossible to make an invisible repair, you can improve the appearance of a chipped joint by applying a tiny droplet of ultraviolet-curing glue to each hole.

Stretch transparent adhesive tape across the repair and rub it down. Leave the glue to cure, then carefully peel off the tape and pare the hardened glue flush with the surface of the glass. Burnish the repair with chrome polish.

Gluing a wineglass stem
Gluing a broken wineglass stem is not easy. Success or failure mostly depends on the shape of the broken edges and whether they lock together without slipping sideways—a problem that is sometimes exacerbated when you introduce glue to the joint. Even when the repair is completely successful, don't be tempted to use the glass for drinking out of.

Supporting the repaired glass
With the glass standing on its rim, glue the repair in the usual way, using ultraviolet-curing adhesive. Support the base of the glass with strips of children's modeling clay while exposing the glue to daylight.

Removing glass stoppers
Although it is not exactly a repair, occasionally most glass collectors are confronted with the problem of having to remove a glass stopper that has become stuck in a decanter or perfume bottle. This usually occurs when the piece has been stored with the stopper in place before the object is completely dry.

The solution is to apply a little bit of olive oil. Apply the oil sparingly around the rim and leave it to seep between the stopper and the neck of the bottle or decanter. Then gingerly twist the stopper to release it.

RESTORING LEADED LIGHTS

Leaded lights are windows that are made from small pieces of textured or colored glass that is held in place by a matrix of grooved lead strips known as cames. Spectacular examples were the glorious features of many Victorian mansions, but by late–Victorian and Edwardian times leaded lights could be produced so cheaply that almost anyone could afford them. As a result, they are frequently found in smaller houses, often in the form of colorful front door panels or bathroom windows.

Any leaded light *in situ* is worth preserving, particularly as many ornamental glass windows were removed during the 1960s and 1970s. Some that were discarded actually survived and have found their way into the hands of antique dealers or, more often, architectural salvage companies, who can arrange to have them installed in your home.

Some collectors treat small leaded panels as works of art and hang them in front of another window where they are displayed to their full advantage.

Supporting a panel
With the window frame laid flat on a work bench, you need to support the horizontal glass-and-lead panel from below. Cut a piece of plywood to fit the opening and cover it with layers of newspaper to fill in the gap.

Repairing leaded lights
It is quite surprising how much restoration work can be done on even badly damaged leaded lights. Usually this is skillful work, and any large-scale restoration that involves resoldering or replacing cames, as well as matching and cutting glass, should be left to an expert. There are professional restorers who will undertake the work for you for very reasonable fees.

It is always worth getting expert advice before embarking on a course of action—but, as long as the panel is accessible and not in a fragile condition, you might consider cleaning a leaded light and perhaps recementing the quarries (individual pieces of glass) to prevent them from rattling.

Working on a workbench
Even leaded lights that are in good condition can be damaged easily unless you treat them carefully. Pressing on the center of a panel, for example, will distort the lead and cause the window to bulge—and if the lead is in poor condition, small pieces of glass may fall out. Consequently it is always advisable to remove a sliding sash window or take a casement window off its hinges, so that you can lay it down flat on a workbench and work on both sides of the panel. You have little choice but to work on a fixed door panel *in situ*, but at least you can reach both sides—be careful not to put too much pressure on the leadwork.

Cleaning leaded lights

Because leaded lights are relatively laborious to keep clean, dirt tends to collect around the edges of the quarries (pieces of glass), and the leadwork becomes covered with white powdery deposits.

1 Cleaning the glass and lead
Unless the glass is etched or sandblasted, wash the lead cames with a soap filled pad, then wipe them clean with a rag and wash the glass with warm, soapy water. Wash a fixed window from the bottom upward, to prevent the dirty water from streaking the glass.

2 Coloring the lead
With a small amount of black lead, fire grate polish on a shoe brush, darken the color of the lead by brushing across the cames (not along them). As long as the glass is clean, fire grate polish will not stick to it, even if the glass is painted. If the glass is not completely clean, wipe off smears of grate polish with a rag that is moistened with white spirit.

Cementing loose quarries

The special cement that is used to hold glass quarries in the cames becomes brittle with age and tends to fall out. Restoring the cement consolidates a window panel and prevents loose quarries from rattling.

1 Preparing the cement
There is no need to buy special cement for a few loose quarries. Press some ordinary glazier's putty between sheets of newspaper to remove some of the oil and knead it into a fairly stiff consistency. Mix in some black fire grate polish until the putty is a dark gray color.

2 Filling in the cames
Using your thumbs, press the putty under the edges of the cames that surround the loose quarries. Remember to fill in both sides of the panel.

3 Removing any excess putty
Sharpen a wooden spatula and use it to scrape any excess polish from around the edges of the glass. Consolidate the putty by brushing across the cames with a shoe brush (see left).

USING AND DISPLAYING GLASS

As long as the glass is not chipped or cracked, there is no reason why you should not use antique glassware for the purpose for which it was intended. The greatest danger is the possibility of accidental damage, especially while you are cleaning glassware after use. Washing each piece carefully by hand (see page 84) reduces the risk considerably.

Long-term storage

Normal household conditions are perfectly safe for storing antique glassware. The ideal storage cabinet has narrow shelves, so that you can see and retrieve every piece without having to reach over other items. Don't lift a glass up by its rim—cup it in your hand and support the base from below.

When storing decanters, do not replace the stoppers. Cover the neck of the decanter with a paper towel that is held in place with a rubber band and store the stopper separately.

A glazed display cabinet is ideal for displaying antique glassware

Displaying glassware in front of a source of light brings out the richness of colored glass and incised decorations

Displaying a collection of glassware

In terms of protection, a glass-fronted display cabinet is probably the ideal place to display antique glassware; but unless the cabinet is lit with a lot of care, cut and engraved glass may not be shown to its full advantage. For this reason alone open shelving is favored by some collectors—but never overcrowd the shelves, and don't risk hanging heavy pictures or mirrors above your glassware collection.

Hanging mirrors

Wall-hung mirrors can be extremely heavy. Always replace the cord; or if the mirror is attached with a chain, check its condition and make sure that it is screwed securely to the back of the mirror.

Mirrored overmantels should stand on the mantel shelf and be screwed into the wall above the fireplace. Metal mirror plates are usually screwed into the frame, close to its top edge. If the plates are missing, examine the back of the mirror for signs of fixings and try to buy suitable replacements.

Backlighting glassware

Displaying glassware in front of a source of light brings out the richness of colored glass and incised decorations. In a display case artificial lighting can be installed behind a translucent back panel, but natural daylight is a cheaper source of illumination.

You can stand glass on a deep windowsill—as long as you do not have to reach across the windowsill to open the window, and there is no possibility of curtains blowing in the breeze. Narrow display shelves running across the front of a stationary light are another alternative; if it is possible, choose windows that do not receive direct sunlight.

Leaded glass panels are obvious candidates for backlighting. Before displaying a panel, have it leaded around the edge by a specialist and ask the restorer to solder strong hooks to the lead so that you can suspend the panel from chains. When you are carrying leaded glass, hold the panel on its edge with both hands; never carry it flat.

Displaying enamels

To provide protection against dust and airborne pollution, display small enameled collectables behind glass—but not in direct sunlight or close to other sources of heat, since fluctuating temperatures can cause the metal backing to expand and contract, with the risk that the enamel may flake off or craze. Don't store enameled pieces in damp or humid conditions, in case the metal corrodes.

Secure an overmantel to the wall with mirror plates

Nineteenth-century enameled buttons in a glass-fronted display case

THE CHARACTER OF WOOD

Patination is the result of various effects and treatments on the surface of a material over a period of time. To a collector, it is a desirable feature, since the patina of age is not easy to reproduce, and so it represents a mark of authenticity. It is also aesthetically pleasing.

The patination of wood varies according to species. Some woods darken with age, others lighten. Ingrained dirt, surface damage, wear marks, and the absorption and accumulation of oil, wax, or other finishes all contribute to the character of the material. It is therefore important to preserve the patina and, where it is possible, to keep cleaning and repair work to a superficial level.

With increased awareness of the need for conservation, many imported exotic woods are now listed as endangered species and are becoming more difficult to find. Rather than dispose of old non-repairable items of woodwork—particularly if they include exotic wood—store them as a valuable source of material for other repair projects. The color of old wood also makes it more suitable than new, unfinished wood for patch repairs.

WOODEN COLLECTABLES

We only have to glance at the wooden objects and artifacts around us to appreciate the variety of indigenous and exotic species that are used to produce all types of functional and decorative handmade and machine-made items. Wood is so versatile as a workable material that it can be used to make items ranging from small, simple artifacts, such as buttons, to magnificent marquetry-covered cabinets and even entire buildings. Indeed, so varied are the properties and appearances of wood that no two pieces—even from the same tree—are ever exactly the same.

In addition to furniture, the chances are that anyone interested in old things is likely to have bought, inherited, or been given items of woodwork, such as clocks, tea caddies, jewelry boxes, gramophones, chess sets, carvings, and wood-framed mirrors or even old woodworking tools for display.

As long as pieces are well cared for, there is no reason why they should not continue to delight collectors for generations to come. You can undertake a number of maintenance tasks yourself—but seek the advice of a specialist restorer if you acquire an important or valuable piece that is in need of restoration or repair.

CLEANING WOOD

Over a period of time dirt that is held by an accumulation of old wax or oil can form a dull film over the surface, masking the rich color and grain of the wood. With careful cleaning, the true colors of the material can be revealed without harming the naturally aged patina. Do not overclean the surfaces or use harsh abrasives, as you risk wearing through the finish. Do not try to remove the darker shading from moldings and carving, as this gives form and character to the decorative details.

Regular cleaning

Dust particles are abrasive and need to be removed regularly with light cleaning. Use a soft cloth duster or dusting mop to dust the surface of sound wood. But don't use a cloth when you are dusting woodwork that has loose or missing moldings, inlay, or veneer, as you may catch and damage the weakened parts: instead use a soft brush. Polish with wax occasionally.

Removing grime
You can buy cleaners for removing dirty accretions of wax, or you can use white spirit. This is safe to use on all finishes and will not harm the grain or the veneer.
  Apply the cleaner with a pad of cloth, working with the grain. Wipe off the residue with a clean cloth or paper towel that is dampened with white spirit and dry with a soft cloth. Finish with a light application of wax polish.

Reviving the finish
After cleaning, check the underlying French polish or varnish finish. If it looks dull but is otherwise sound, you can revitalize it with a burnishing cream, that is specifically made for polishing furniture, or with any mildly abrasive cleaner, such as car paint cleaner or metal polish. Apply the reviver with a soft cloth and use firm pressure as you burnish the surface. Finish with a light protective coating of fine wax.

IDENTIFYING THE FINISH

In order to refurbish an old, polished surface, it is necessary to identify the type of finish. Traditional finishes for wood include oil, wax, French polish, cellulose lacquer, and oil-based varnishes. Some modern varnishes are acrylic-based. The formulation of the finishes may vary, particularly ones of modern manufacture—although these are not likely to be encountered on antique pieces unless they have been refinished recently.

  Wax, French polish, cellulose lacquer, and acrylic varnish are reversible by dissolving them with the appropriate solvent. White spirit will dissolve wax. Methylated spirit and acetone will dissolve French polish. Acetone or cellulose thinners will also dissolve cellulose lacquer or acrylic varnish. Oil-based finishes are non-reversible, however, and they are not affected by common solvents. These varnishes require the application of a chemical to soften them.

  To test which finish is used, apply each solvent in turn with a white cloth. Work on a hidden part of the surface. The softened polish will leave a telltale mark on the cloth.

Caring for woodwork

To avoid the damaging effects of strong sunlight, change the position of wooden items that are placed near a window. Where it is possible, keep wood out of direct sunlight.

  Keep items away from radiators, since central heating can cause wood to dry out excessively, which leads to shrinkage problems. Use place mats and coasters to protect polished tabletops—particularly those with French-polished surfaces—from hot crockery and spillage from drinking glasses. Wipe off any spilled liquids immediately.

  Attend to worn fittings, such as hinges or castors, before aany damage is caused to other components.

  Inspect newly acquired pieces of old woodwork carefully for signs of furniture beetle (woodworm) infestation, so you do not inadvertently introduce the problem into your home. Treat with an insecticide.

REMOVING SURFACE MARKS

Wood is a porous material that will absorb dirt and grease if it is not given a protective finish. However, traditional surface finishes can be marked by water, alcohol, and other liquids such as ink. Heat can also mark up the finish.

Some marks are only superficial and can be rubbed out easily; others may require the finish to be stripped and the wood to be refinished. Before undertaking remedial work, consider whether it is really necessary, since accumulated marks form part of the patina. However, if the marks are disfiguring, it may be better to remove them.

Removing white marks
White marks, often in the form of rings or round patches, are typically found in non-penetrating finishes such as French polish. The marks are usually only on the surface of the polish and have been caused either by water or by a hot plate or cup being placed directly onto the surface. Remove the resulting white bloom by rubbing gently with a mildly abrasive cleaner applied with a soft cloth. Be careful not to rub through the finish, or you will need to rebuild it locally.

Removing etched marks
Spilled alcohol or cosmetic solvents can etch deep marks into the finish if they are left in contact with the polished surface. Try disguising the damage by treating it with a mildly abrasive cleaner. Alternatively, try reworking the finish with a pad that is dampened with the appropriate solvent, in order to even out the damaged surface.

If this proves to be insufficient, you will need to rebuild the finish. Carefully remove the polish with more solvent to form a patch with feathered edges, then leave it to dry. Apply the appropriate polish to the patch with a brush and leave it to harden. Rub it down with very fine abrasive paper and finish with a burnishing cream.

Dealing with scratches
Old scratches are an indication of wear and tear over the years, so they may add to the character of a piece. However, you can rub out fine scratches, using a mildly abrasive cleaner applied with a soft cloth. Alternatively, disguise the scratches with a proprietary liquid retoucher. Apply it liberally over the scratched area and leave it to dry for an hour or so, then remove the excess and polish it with a soft cloth.

Using wax filler
Treat deeper scratches with a proprietary wood-colored wax stick. These are made in a range of shades to blend in with different woods. Rub the stick across the scratch to fill in the recess. Wipe off the surplus and burnish the surface with a soft cloth. If it is necessary, finish with a wax polish.

Filling in deep scratches
Fill in deep scratches in French polish or varnish with a compatible finish. Use varnish straight from the can, but pour a small amount of French polish into a small dish and allow it to thicken. Apply the finish liberally along the scratch, using a fine artist's paintbrush. Build up the finish, leaving it to set between applications, until it is above the surface level. Leave it to harden fully, then carefully scrape off the surplus and finish flush with very fine abrasive paper followed by burnishing cream.

REPAIRING THE SURFACE

In the same way that scratches often add character to old wood, other blemishes can too, such as dents, splits, scorch marks, and wormholes.

A measure of their worth can be gauged by the fact that makers of reproduction furniture "distress" new pieces with hot irons, chains, and metal bars in order to produce an aged look. Before embarking on repairs, assess whether they really are desirable. Considerations of value aside, if the damage disfigures an otherwise good surface, repairs are justified.

Using shellac sticks
Shellac sticks are a harder form of filler that are ideal for repairing larger holes. Use a soldering iron to melt the shellac into the hole. Overfill the hole and, while the shellac is still soft, press it into place with a metal blade heated in warm water. When the filler has set, pare or scrape it flush with the surface and, if need be, sand it with fine abrasive paper.

Repairing small holes and splits
Use colored-wax sticks to repair wormholes and fine splits. These are made in a range of shades to approximate the color of the most common woods.

Knead a piece of the wax between your fingers to soften it, then press it into the holes with a filling knife. Scrape off any excess filler once it has hardened and burnish with the back of a piece of abrasive paper. Finish by applying wax or French polish.

Raising dents
Impact from a hard object or pressure from a heavy weight can cause the cell structure of wood to be crushed. To remove the resulting depression, use a small artist's paintbrush to apply drops of hot water to the damaged area. The wood will gradually swell back to its original level as the water is absorbed. Repeat the process if necessary and, when the wood is fully dry, sand the swollen fibers smooth.

If the application of water is not sufficient, try steam. Place a damp cloth over the dent and heat it with a soldering iron. The steam should quickly cause the fibers to swell.

REMOVING DEEP SCRATCHES AND BURNS

Deep scratches across the grain or burn marks from a cigarette are usually regarded as unacceptable. Depending on the depth, it may be possible to erase the damage with abrasive paper or by using a sharp cabinet scraper. In either case you will be removing the surface of the wood and will therefore need to use a wood dye to blend in the color of the exposed wood.

When you are using abrasives, start with the least coarse grade necessary and work through to the finer grades. Always work along the grain—never across it—as fine cross-grain scratches will be highlighted by the final finish.

Use a cabinet scraper for quicker results and more control over a small area. Start by working the scraper diagonally across the grain from opposite sides, then finish following the grain. Although it is not always necessary after scraping, you may need to sand the surface with a fine abrasive paper to prepare it for finishing.

Filling holes and dents
Deep burn mark, woodworm, or impact damage may mean that the wood has to be patch-repaired. The new wood will require careful finishing to blend in with the original material.

1 Cutting a surface patch
The best way to fix a deep blemish in the surface of a panel is to inlay a thick piece of matching wood that has beem selected for color and grain. Cut a diamond-shaped patch that will cover the damaged area, with the long axis following the grain. Plane a slight taper on each edge of the patch.

2 Cutting the recess
Hold the patch over the damage and mark around it with a sharp pencil. Carefully chisel out the waste, leaving a tapered recess that is slightly shallower than the thickness of the patch.

3 Fitting the patch
Test the fit as you work. Once the patch is a close fit, apply PVA adhesive into the recess and to the patch. Tap the patch into place, wipe off excess glue, and, when the glue has set, plane the surface flush. Sand the surface so that it is ready for finishing.

REPAIRING A BROKEN EDGE

If an integral molding has broken off and is missing, you have little choice but to graft on a new piece and shape it *in situ*. First smooth off the broken edge using a block plane, then prepare a patch of matching wood that is slightly oversized and glue it into place. Use self-adhesive tape to hold it in place if clamping is difficult.

When the glue has set, shape the contour with hand planes, chisels, and gouges, as required, then bring it to its final shape with abrasive paper. Where it is possible, make a shaped sanding block to follow the contour.

STRIPPING WOOD

Stripping the finish off old or collectable woodwork should only be done as a last resort, since a lot of the character and value will be lost. However, there are times—following fire damage, for example—when you have little choice. Small items that are polished with reversible finishes can be gently stripped with the appropriate solvent. Use white spirit to clean off wax, methylated spirit to remove French polish, and cellulose thinners for cellulose lacquers. Apply the solvent liberally with pads of very fine wire wool, working with the grain.

Using proprietary strippers

If you are faced with stripping a large area of wood, or when time is short, use a fast-acting commercial chemical stripper. You can buy a variety of types from building suppliers. General-purpose strippers—available in liquid, gel, or paste form—are formulated to react with virtually all paint and wood finishes. Strippers for removing tough varnishes are also made. Most strippers contain harmful chemicals, so they require careful handling—but this does not need to be a problem, as long as you follow the manufacturer's directions carefully. There are also "safe" strippers that do not irritate the skin or give off strong fumes.

When it comes to washing off the chemical residues, you have a choice between strippers that use water or white spirit. Choose one that uses white spirit, as this will not harm the grain nor unduly affect the adhesion of the veneers. Before using commercial strippers, contact your local community center to find out about facilities for disposing of chemical wastes.

1 Applying chemical stripper

Read and follow the manufacturer's instructions carefully. Wear a face mask, goggles, protective gloves, and, since it is messy work, old clothes. Pour some stripper into a jar or foil dish. Using an old paintbrush, liberally coat the surface with stripper. Leave it for up to 15 minutes to soften the finish, then test the penetration with a scraper. If the finish has not softened down to the wood, apply more stripper and stipple the blistered coating back into contact with the surface.

2 Removing the waste

When the finish is fully softened, use a paint scraper to remove the residue from flat surfaces. Work along the grain, not across it. Wipe the waste from the blade onto sheets of newspaper for safe disposal.

3 Dealing with shaped work

Use a sharpened stick to remove heavy waste deposits from moldings and carved details. Follow this with balls of fine wire wool, turning them inside out as they get clogged—but use a nylon-fiber pad impregnated with abrasive particles when you are cleaning oak, since natural acids in the wood can react with trapped particles of wire, causing black stains. Use pads of wire wool (nylon-fiber pads for oak) to clean shaped parts that have been turned on a lathe.

4 Cleaning the surface

Clean the remainder of the stripper from the surface and pores of the wood with pads that are dipped in fresh stripper, rubbing in the direction of the grain. Wash off all traces of stripper with white spirit, applied with a cloth. Leave the wood to dry before preparing it for refinishing.

Dealing with furniture beetle

The discovery of furniture beetle (or woodworm) in old wood tends to alarm many people —sometimes to such an extent that they may consider destroying the piece to stop the infestation from spreading. However, that is rarely necessary. Certainly an infestation should not be ignored, but as long as it is attended to promptly, it can be contained and reinfestation can be prevented by simple methods.

Checking for woodworm

Holes about ⅛ inch (2mm) in size in the surface of the wood are likely to be the first signs of furniture beetle infestation. However, it is the beetle's larvae that cause the real damage as they burrow through the wood.

The life cycle begins with the female beetle laying its eggs on rough, unfinished surfaces or in other convenient crevices. When they hatch, the larvae proceed to burrow deep into the wood to feed, leaving a maze of tunnels behind them. After pupating just below the surface, they emerge as beetles, leaving the telltale holes.

Inspect all the surfaces of the wood for such holes—paying close attention to hidden parts, where activity may escape notice. Dark-colored holes are likely to be the remains of an old, and now dormant, outbreak. Light-colored holes could indicate a fresh attack. Check for signs of fine dust on the surface on which the piece is standing. This could be "frass" (chewed wood waste produced by the larvae), which would indicate recent activity.

Eradicating woodworm

You can buy woodworm-treatment fluid from most hardware stores—either in large cans for applying with a brush or in aerosol sprays or in an applicator for injecting into the holes. Follow the manufacturer's instructions when you are using these chemicals. Protect your eyes with goggles, particularly when using the injection method, and wear protective gloves.

Injecting the fluid
Insert the nozzle of the applicator into the holes and inject the fluid until it runs out. It is not necessary to treat every hole, as the chambers are usually interconnected. For this reason do not lean over the piece you are working on while injecting the fluid, as it can spurt out from another hole. Wipe off any excess fluid from finished surfaces.

Testing the wood
A large number of holes indicates a serious attack—but as long as the wood is not weakened structurally, it can be saved.

Probe the infected area with a sharp, pointed blade. If the wood offers no resistance or crumbles under pressure, it needs to be replaced. If the wood feels solid, it can be treated with a chemical insecticide.

Brush applications
Use a brush to treat large areas of unfinished wood. Pour fluid into a dish and coat the surfaces liberally. Allow it to soak in and repeat the application when the surface has dried.

Treat new wood in this way to prevent future infestations. You can apply any finish to the wood once it is dry. Also, as a preventative measure, you can maintain the finished surface with an insecticidal wax polish that is available from specialist suppliers.

BLEACHING WOOD

Persistent stains that are left in the fibers of the wood after stripping the finish will require the use of bleach to remove them. Bleach can also be used to modify the natural color of the wood, should that be necessary when you are including new wood as part of a repair. You can make your own bleaching solution using oxalic acid crystals or buy a proprietary two-part bleach.

Using oxalic acid crystals

Oxalic acid is a traditional bleach for removing stains without altering the natural color of the wood. It is also the most effective for removing black iron stains that are caused by tannins in woods, such as oak, reacting with ironwork. You can buy it as crystals from drugstores or restoration suppliers. Handle it with care, since the crystals are toxic. Wear a mask, goggles, and gloves while you are using oxalic acid—both in dry and liquid form—and ventilate the workshop. Prepare the solution in a glass jar or plastic pot (do not use a metal container) half filled with warm water. Make a saturated solution by adding the crystals to the water, stirring gently, until no more will dissolve. Never pour water onto the crystals; always add them to the water.

Applying the bleach

Using a nylon or white-fiber brush, apply the bleach to the stained area and leave it to form a crystalline film as it dries. If the stain persists, you may need to apply more bleach before leaving the wood to dry.

Rinse off and neutralize the bleach with washes of clean water. Wipe away the excess water and leave it to dry. As the water will have raised the grain, lightly sand the surface smooth. Wear a face mask.

Lightening the color

To change the natural color of wood to a lighter tone (as well as for lifting stubborn stains), use a strong two-part bleach. The degree to which the color changes will depend on the nature of the wood and the time that is allowed for the bleach to work. Where it is possible, make a test on a spare piece of similar wood or on a hidden part of the work.

Using bleach

Following the manufacturer's instructions carefully, apply the first agent to the wood with a brush. Leave it for around five to ten minutes (the wood may turn a darker color), then apply the second solution.

Allow the bleach to work. As soon as the wood reaches the required color, stop the action by neutralizing the bleach with a wash of weak acetic acid made from one teaspoonful of white vinegar in one pint of water. Sand the surface of the wood once it is dry. Wear a face mask.

TYPES OF WOOD DYES

Wood dyes penetrate deep into the fibers of the wood and modify the natural color, but they are not a finish in themselves. All penetrating dyes need to be protected with a surface finish. Some finishes, such as prestained varnishes, contain a coloring to achieve a similar appearance, but the color mostly remains in the surface film and is lost when the finish is removed.

Traditional penetrating dyes are supplied as powdered pigments for mixing with the appropriate solvent. This offers the widest choice for color matching, but it takes experience to achieve the right mix. Ready-mixed dyes are easier to use and are available in a range of common wood shades.

Compatibility

You can mix practically any wood shade using compatible wood dyes or stains—as well as lightening the color by adding more of the appropriate thinner. When choosing a stain, select one that will not be reactivated by the solvent in the finish that you need to apply, causing the color to bleed or become mobile as you work on the surface.

Seal a solvent stain with shellac or sanding sealer before applying a varnish, lacquer, or wax polish that is thinned with white spirit, turpentine, or cellulose thinner. Use a spirit dye for any finish other than French polish. Water-based stains can be used with any finish, but test the results on a hidden part first if you are planning to apply acrylic varnish.

COLORING WOOD

Blending the color of new work with the old is one of the most difficult tasks when repairing woodwork. It is made even more difficult by the fact that any new finish, even if it is as clear as water, tends to darken the coloring.

To ensure a close match, it is best to make up a color-sample strip, using a piece cut from the patch material. Various tests can be tried—by only applying the appropriate finish or wood dyes of differing strengths covered with the finish. Hold the sample strip against the work to judge the most suitable color-and-tone combination. Err on the lighter side, as you can darken the color slightly with a colored-wax dressing.

Applying penetrating wood dyes

Set up an uncluttered work station, according to the size of the piece, in a well-ventilated, dust-free area. Wear PVC gloves and an apron—and old clothes if you are dyeing a large piece. You can apply wood dyes using a good-quality paintbrush, a decorator's mohair pile paint pad, or a wad of soft cloth. If you have a compressor or airbrush kit, you can spray them on.

Staining the end grain
The open cells of the end grain absorb more stain and will therefore appear darker than the other parts of the wood. To counteract this, partially seal the end grain with a brush coat of white shellac or sanding sealer. This will reduce the amount of color that is taken up by the edge of the wood. Allow it to dry fully before staining.

Preparing the surface
Bring the surface to a fine sanded finish—making sure that there are no cross-grain scratches or rough fibers, which would absorb more stain, resulting in a patchy finish. If need be, wet the surface with clean water to raise the grain, then sand smooth when it is dry. This is essential before applying a water-based stain. Ensure that no glue remains on the surface, as this can affect the absorption of the stain.

Staining carved wood
Apply the stain with a soft brush, working it well into the carved details while immediately absorbing any surplus coloring from the hollows with a paper towel or cloth rag.

Applying the stain
Pour enough stain to cover the repair into a shallow dish. Brush or swab the stain onto the wood in the direction of the grain, blending in the wet edges when you are working over a large area. Allow it to soak in, then evenly wipe off any surplus stain with a clean cloth pad.

COLORING VENEERS

Veneers bonded with watersoluble animal glue can be colored best with solvent or spirit-based stain. You can use any type of stain for veneers that are bonded with other glues. Apply the stain as you would for solid wood.

For a patch repair or a piece of marquetry, color the veneer before gluing it into place. Dip the pieces into the stain to obtain an even coloring and leave them to dry before cutting to the right size and shape.

REPLACING AND REPAIRING THE FINISH

Wood is usually treated with a finish to enhance its appearance and provide a protective coating. The finish also helps stabilize the wood, as it renders it less able to pull in moisture.

The type of finish will depend on the nature of the wood and how it is used. Most finishes are translucent, in order to allow the color and grain of the wood to be seen, but opaque paints are sometimes used to decorate and disguise poorer quality woods.

Traditional translucent wood finishes include wax, oil finishes, oil-based varnish, and shellac-based French polish.

Wax polish

Wax has a long history as a finish for wood. It can be used as a finish in itself or as a dressing to maintain the surface of other finishes, such as French polish and varnish. It is not a tough finish, but it is simple to apply and maintain—and over a period of many years it imparts a mellow quality that looks particularly attractive on old wood.

Types of wax polishes
You can buy the raw materials for making traditional wax polishes from specialist suppliers, but it is more convenient to use one of the many ready-made, natural wax products that are now available. Pale waxes in semiliquid cream or nonliquid paste form give a beautiful, mellow finish to light colored woods, while the darker-colored "antique" waxes produce a richer coloring for old sun-bleached woods and finishes. Microcrystalline waxes are fine, clear waxes that do not stain even the lightest woods; they are used by conservators to protect and enhance a great many materials.

1 Applying a cream finish
Apply a brush coat of shellac or cellulose sealer to bare wood and rub it down with fine silicon-carbide paper when it is dry. Pour the semiliquid cream wax into a foil dish and use a soft paintbrush to apply a liberal coating to the surface. Leave this coating to harden for around an hour.

2 Building up the polish
Apply a second coat with a soft cloth pad, working across the surface with an overlapping spiral action, then finish following the grain. Allow the wax to harden again and repeat if necessary. Using a clean, soft polishing cloth, vigorously buff the surface in the direction of the grain to bring out the shine.

1 Using paste wax
Prepare and seal the wood as you would for a cream wax. Load the face of a cloth pad with paste wax wiped from the can. Work the cloth along the grain with a circular action, finishing with straight strokes.

2 Building up the polish
Use a ball of fine 0000-grade wire wool or a nylon-fiber pad impregnated with fine abrasive particles to apply another coat of wax around 20 minutes after the first. Work the pad along the grain only. Leave the wax to harden and repeat to build up a protective coating. Finally, buff firmly with a soft cloth or use a wax-polishing brush. A brush makes polishing carved work easier.

Using microcrystalline wax
Apply the wax sparingly with a soft cotton cloth. Use a brush for carved surfaces. Polish the surface with a clean cloth immediately after application.

Oil finishes

Oil finishes have been used for a long time to preserve and enhance the beauty of wood. They are easy to apply, producing a lustrous interior or exterior finish that does not need much maintenance. Traditional linseed oil is still available for an authentic finish for old wood, but because it dries slowly, it has now mostly been superseded by faster-drying, hard-wearing modern alternatives. Gelled oil, a modern blend of natural oils and synthetic resin, has the consistency of soft wax polish.It can be applied to bare wood and, unlike other oil finishes, may be applied over existing lacquer and varnish finishes.

Oiling wood
Pour the oil into a foil dish and use a soft paintbrush to apply an even, liberal coat of the finish. Leave the oil to be absorbed before wiping the excess from the surface with a soft cloth. Allow it to dry, then around six hours later apply a second coat and leave it to dry overnight. Follow this with another coat, this time applied with a cloth pad. When it is dry, burnish with a soft cloth.

Oils that dry by oxidation give off heat as they dry, which can cause soiled cloths to ignite spontaneously. As a safety precaution, either soak oily cloths in water overnight or leave them unfolded to dry in the open air before you dispose of them.

Applying gelled oil
Apply gelled oil to bare wood with a cloth pad, rubbing it vigorously in the direction of the grain until it is dry to the touch. Apply two or more coats (depending on how hard-wearing it needs to be), allowing each application to dry for around four hours. Leave the finish to dry to a soft sheen. Over existing non-penetrative finishes, only apply a light coat of gelled oil.

Varnishing wood

Traditional oil varnish is a blend of natural resins, oil, and solvent. Modern oil varnishes use synthetic materials. Oil varnishes—also known as solvent-based varnishes—dry by oxidation. As the solvent evaporates, the oxygen from the air is absorbed by the oil, causing a chemical change that prevents the dried finish from being reactivated by the solvent. Brushes must therefore be washed in solvent before the varnish dries.

The latest variants use acrylic resins and are water based. These have certain advantages over oil-based finishes, as they are nontoxic and practically odorless. They dry quickly and are non-yellowing and nonflammable. After use, brushes can be washed out in water. Although acrylic varnishes are not a traditional finish for old woodwork, their properties make them worth considering for renewing a stripped surface.

Applying varnish
Varnish can be applied with a soft brush in the same way as paint; it is, in fact, virtually the same material but without the opaque pigments that are present in paints. Use a good-quality, natural-bristle brush for oil varnishes and a nylon-fiber brush for acrylic varnishes.

Applying a sealer coat
For sealing bare wood, thin out oil-based varnish by ten percent. Apply the varnish evenly with a brush. When the surface is dry, rub it down with fine wet-and-dry paper that is dipped in water, then wipe it clean, using a cloth dampened with white spirit.

Apply acrylic varnish full strength and rub it down when it is dry. Do not use wire wool to rub down acrylic varnishes, as tiny slivers of metal can get trapped in the surface, causing black spots in the next coat. Wipe the surface with a cloth that is dampened with water.

Brushing the varnish
Brush on oil varnish following the grain of the wood, then work across it to spread the coating out evenly. Working relatively quickly, brush toward the edge that you have just finished, in order to blend the wet edges. Finally, "lay off" along the grain with very light brushstrokes. Leave the varnish to set, then rub it down before applying a second coat.

Apply acrylic varnish liberally across the grain and then lay off following the grain. When the surface is dry, after around 30 minutes, rub it down and apply a second or third coat.

FRENCH POLISHING

Made from shellac that has been dissolved in methylated spirit, French polish produces a high-gloss finish that enhances the color and beauty of the wood. It was particularly popular in Victorian times, when it was widely used for finishing close-grained woods such as mahogany, walnut, and satinwood. Despite its look of quality, French polish is not a hard-wearing finish and can be marked easily.

French polishing has always been regarded as a job for specialists, since producing the perfect finish requires skills that can only be developed with practice. However, the process only uses basic materials, and it is possible for a patient and competent craftsperson to achieve a satisfactory result. To begin withm it is essential that the wood is perfectly smooth, and the polish needs to be applied in thin layers over a period of days.

Preparing the work area

All polishing processes require a dust-free atmosphere—and none more so than French polishing. You also need to work in a dry, warm room. Where it is possible, work in front of a window or a well-illuminated area so that the light falls across the surface of the piece.

You will need to make a pad for applying the polish and will need to have to hand some fine silicon-carbide abrasive paper, light lubricating oil, a soft brush, and burnishing cream. If making a patch repair, choose the type of polish best suited to the colour of the wood or existing finish.

Making a pad
The traditional method for applying French polish is to use a pad that is made from cotton or fine linen cloth filled with cotton wadding.

Make the pad a suitable size—so that it fits neatly in the palm of your hand—and is roughly pointed in shape, so that you can work polish into corners.

Holding the wrapped pad in one hand, twist the gathered ends of the covering with the other, in order to compress the pad. Fold the twisted tail over and onto the back of the pad to form a grip that fits into your hand and leaves a smooth sole to the pad.

Charging the pad
Once you have mastered the art of wrapping the pad, hold it unfolded in one hand. Pour some polish into the wadding, squeezing it gently until it is wet all the way through but not saturated. Refold the covering and press the sole of the pad against a clean, flat surface to distribute the polish evenly. Squeeze out the surplus. You will need to repeat this process as the polish is used up.

Storing a pad
To keep the pad clean and prevent it from drying out, keep it in an airtight screw-top jar between applications. Stored in this way the pad will remain supple for months, and you will not need to discard it until the cloth has worn through.

Traditional wood finishers usually reuse the old wadding for applying French polish as a preparatory wood sealer.

BRUSHING SHELLAC

For jobs that do not warrant the laborious traditional French polish treatment, time-saving brushing shellacs are available. These are specially formulated for brush application, as they flow easily and are slower drying in order to avoid brush marks. The wood needs to be prepared in the same way as for traditional French polishing.

1 Applying the polish
Load a soft brush with polish and apply it using straight, even strokes, following the grain. Work relatively quickly to avoid dragging the wet edge of the previous stroke. Use a light touch at the edges, since it is easy to wipe off too much shellac from the brush, causing runs. Brush out any runs as they occur.

Allow around an hour for the surface to dry, then rub it down with fine silicon-carbide paper. Apply one or two more coats in the same way.

2 Finishing with wax
A well-prepared surface should result in a bright-gloss finish. If you want a more subtle glow, apply a wax polish with a pad of fine wire wool, working evenly along the grain. As brush-applied shellac builds up to a good thickness, there is little risk of rubbing through—but do not overrub the surface, just in case. Buff with a soft cloth.

Applying French polish

French polish produces a high-gloss finish that highlights any flaws in the surface. Therefore it is essential to prepare the wood thoroughly before polishing. The method explained here is for finishing a stripped flat surface.

Preparing the surface

Fill in any surface damage (see pages 96–97) and sand the wood smooth; if it is required, apply a wood dye to color the wood (see page 101). If you are treating new wood that has an open grain, you will need to fill in the pores to create a smooth surface. This can be achieved by successive coats of French polish, which have to be rubbed down inbetween applications, or by the less laborious application of a grain filler.

1 Applying a grain filler

Ready-mixed grain filler pastes are available in a range of wood colors. Choose one that closely matches the color of the wood. Make sure that the surface is clean and free from dust, then apply the filler with a pad of coarse cloth. Work it into the grain using overlapping circular strokes.

When it is almost dry, rub across the grain with a clean pad of coarse cloth to remove the excess filler. Use a sharp stick to clean filler out from the corners and moldings. Leave it to harden overnight, then sand lightly.

Filling in stained wood

Applying filler over a ready-stained surface may result in some color being removed when the surface is sanded; but if you fill it in first, there is a possibility that the absorption will vary, resulting in an uneven coloring. To overcome this problem, apply the stain first, then protect it with a brush coat of sanding sealer or transparent French polish, followed by the grain filler mixed with a little of the compatible wood dye.

1 Applying a sealer coat

Remove any dust from the surface of the wood, using a vacuum cleaner with a brush attachment. Charge the pad with thinned French polish and apply the first coat lightly, with long, overlapping strokes following the grain, to seal the wood. As the work progresses, increase the pressure —to encourage the polish to flow. Cover the surface, keeping the pad moving, and do not go back over the work.

Leave the sealer coat to harden for around an hour, then rub it down with very fine silicon-carbide paper. Apply and rub down another coat if the first one is uneven.

2 Bodying up the polish

"Bodying up" is the process of applying thin layers of shellac to build up the polish. Charge the pad with full strength polish; then, using a continuous movement and overlapping, circular strokes, cover the entire surface with polish. Do not allow the pad to rest on the surface, as it can stick and scar the polish. At the edges sweep the pad off the work.

3 Using different strokes

To help build up an even coating, start again and apply some more polish—this time using a figure eight movement. Follow this by using overlapping, parallel strokes along the surface. Leave it to dry for around 30 minutes, then repeat the whole process to build up three or four layers.

4 Lubricating the pad

Depending on the size of the work, it may be necessary to recharge the pad with polish as the work progresses. As the finish builds up, the pad may begin to drag on the new surface. To overcome this, apply a small amount of linseed oil on the sole to lubricate the pad, then continue as before. Use the oil sparingly.

After building up the finish, leave the polish to harden overnight. Repeat the process over a period of days, until you are satisfied with the condition of the surface.

5 Removing the oil

At this stage the builtup surface is likely to display dull streaks. This is the residue of the lubricating oil. To remove it, add a little methylated spirit to an almost polish-free pad and squeeze it almost dry. Sweep the pad across the work with straight parallel strokes, gradually increasing the pressure until the pad begins to drag. Leave it to dry for a few minutes; then repeat the process until the streaking disappears, leaving a high gloss. Leave it to harden for around a week.

6 Burnishing the surface

If you are not satisfied with the final gloss, you can polish the hard surface with a special-purpose burnishing cream. Apply the cream with a soft cloth, rubbing vigorously, then polish it to a deep shine with a clean, soft cloth.

VENEERS

Veneer is a thin sheet of decorative wood that has been bonded to a structural backing panel known as the groundwork. The groundwork of older pieces of veneered woodwork is generally made from solid pine or mahogany. Used properly, these woods provide a good base for veneers—but, like all solid woods, they are affected by atmospheric conditions, which often leads to a breakdown of the veneered surface. Today stable, man-made boards are used.

To distinguish veneered work from solid wood, look at the edges of panels to see if the grain of the wood is continuous. Also, check the underside or inside of the work to see if the wood is the same as the surface.

Although it is more susceptible to damage, veneer offers the use of exotic and unusual woods that would be impractical if they were used in solid form. Also, the grain of the wood can be varied according to the method that is used for cutting the veneer—giving an even greater choice of pattern, which craftspeople have successfully exploited for centuries.

Repairing veneered surfaces

Well-laid veneer should provide a trouble-free surface that can be maintained in a similar way to solid wood. However, it is less tolerant of moisture and changes in humidity.

Traditionally veneer work was done using watersoluble animal glue and laid by hand with a veneer hammer or in a press. Animal glue is reversible with the application of heat and moisture and is preferred by professional restorers, although modern glues can be used for some repairs.

Most problems with veneered surfaces are caused by a breakdown of the glue, resulting in blisters or splintered edges. Poorly made or inadequately prepared groundwork can also lead to cross-grain fractures. In the latter case it is usually necessary to remove, repair, and relay the old veneer or to replace it. The groundwork will also need attention. If you are in any doubt about your own abilities, take restoration work of this type to a professional.

Treating blisters

Blisters are particularly disfiguring on a polished surface, as they are highlighted by the gloss finish. Sometimes an area of loose veneer, caused by a lack of glue, can be less obvious. To detect a patch that has become detached, tap the surface with your fingernails and listen for a hollow sound. As the treatment requires the application of water and heat, it will be necessary to remove the surface finish (see page 98).

1 Flattening a blister
First try flattening the blister by reactivating the old glue. Place a damp cloth over the veneer and apply heat with an electric iron. The heat and moisture should soften the glue as well as the veneer, making it more pliable.

2 Clamping the repair
Press the veneer flat and then cover it with a piece of polyethylene plastic sheeting and a flat block of wood. Apply pressure with a clamp or heavy weight until the glue has set.

3 Adding glue
If insufficient glue was used in the first place, make a slit with a sharp knife along the blister, following the grain. Soften the veneer (as above) and work hot animal glue under the veneer with a brush. Press it flat and wipe away any surplus glue with a damp cloth, then cover and press the repair flat.

Repairing damaged edges

The edges of veneered surfaces, crossbanded border,s and edge lippings are susceptible to damage and frequently require repairs. Choose a veneer that closely matches the grain of the original wood. The color can be modified, if need be, when the surface finish is applied (see page 101). The patch veneer needs to be slightly thicker than the surface veneer to allow for final sanding.

Repairing crossbanded borders

Crossbanding is used to create a decorative border around a veneered panel. A matching or contrasting veneer may be used, cut into strips with the grain running across the width of the banding.

Having "short" grain,cross-banded borders can be chipped easily. They can be patch-repaired—or if they are badly damaged, they can be replaced.

1 Patching the edge
Cut the selected patch veneer slightly larger than the damaged area. Be careful to match up the grain as well as possible and tape it in place over the damaged portion. Using a knife and metal ruler, make angled cuts through both veneers to form the patch and cutout.

1 Patching the border
Tape an oversized piece of selected veneer over the damaged border. Make cuts that are square to the edge, through both veneers, on each side of the damage, using a knife and ruler. Make a cut that is parallel to the edge between the two cuts, following the inner banding line.

2 Preparing the cutout
Remove the patch and, using a sharp chisel, carefully trim away the remnants of the original splintered veneer from the groundwork. Dampening the waste can make it easier to remove. Scrape the surface smooth with a chisel held upright.

2 Fitting the patch
Remove the patch and, if need be, recut the lines in the border. Chisel out the waste from the cutout and scrape the groundwork smooth. Apply glue to the cutout and veneer. Tape the patch into place and clamp it flat, using a block. When it has set, trim it to size and sand the veneer.

3 Gluing the patch
Apply hot animal glue or a modern cold-setting PVA woodworking adhesive to the patch and groundwork. Position the patch and hold it in place with gummed paper tape. Press it flat with a wooden block that is lined with polyethylene sheeting and held in a clamp. When the glue has set, trim off the waste from the edge, holding the panel face down on a flat surface. Sand it so that it is ready for finishing.

Patching the surface
Damage to the main surface of the veneer, such as a burn mark, can be patched in a similar way to an edge repair. Tape an oversized patch of the selected veneer over the damaged area. Be careful to align the grain. Cut a "boat-shaped" patch through both veneers. Trim the waste from the cutout and glue the patch into place. If the groundwork is also damaged, cut and fit a plug (see page 97) before patching.

INLAY AND MARQUETRY

Inlay is an intricate technique in which contrasting colored woods—in the form of stringings, decorative veneer bandings, or marquetry motifs—are set into recesses that are cut into a solid panel.

Stringings are single strips of solid wood that are made in a limited range of square and flat sections. They are used to outline decorative panels or borders and are produced in "white" and "black" versions to contrast with the surrounding wood.

Decorative bandings are veneer-thick strips that are made in various widths and patterns from a variety of exotic and colored woods.

Marquetry motifs are made from various natural and colored veneers that are cut and assembled to form ornate floral and naturalistic designs. Parquetry, a form of marquetry, is made from veneers that are cut into geometric shapes. Marquetry and parquetry designs may be inlaid or made up and laid as a single sheet of veneer.

On antique items you will often find that pieces of inlay have become loose or are missing due to the movement of the groundwork. Loose pieces can be reglued, but missing pieces will need to be remade. Ready-made decorative bandings and marquetry motifs in traditional designs are available from veneer suppliers.

Fitting stringing
Clean the groove that is left by the missing stringing, using a narrow chisel, knife blade, or bradawl. Dry fit the selected stringing into the groove and mark the required length. If the groove follows a curve, dampening the stringing will help make it bend. Cut the stringing to the correct length, apply animal glue into the groove, and press the stringing into place with a cross-peen hammer.

Repairing the edge stringing
Clean the rebate that is left by the missing stringing with a sharp chisel held upright or use a scratch stock. Apply glue and press the prepared stringing into place. Use short lengths of masking tape wrapped over the edge to hold the stringing while the glue sets.

Repairing decorative banding

Parts of the decorative elements that make up the banding may be missing. If they are insignificant, try filling in the gap with a colored-wax or shellac stick filler. Where most of the banding is missing, you may be able to patch-repair the damaged strip, as long as you can find a ready-made banding to match. If not, it may be necessary to replace the strip with one that closely resembles the original.

Replacing the banding
Scrape the groove with a sharp chisel to remove dirt, old wax, and glue. Trim the broken end of the original banding square, then chisel out the waste. Match the pattern and cut the new banding to the correct length. Glue it into place and press it down with a cross-peen hammer.

PREPARING ANIMAL GLUE

Traditional animal glue is available in bead form from craft suppliers. It is prepared for use in a double or jacketed glue pot—or you can improvise by using a clean food can placed in a small pan.

Fill the glue pot a quarter full with glue beads, cover them with hot water, and leave it to soak. Place the glue pot in the pan and half fill the pan with water. Heat the water to soften the glue, making sure that the glue does not boil. Stir it regularly and add hot water as required, until the glue has a smooth, easy-flowing consistency.

Repairing marquetry and parquetry

Decorative marquetry and parquetry panels featuring complex designs that are in need of repair should be left to a professional restorer. However, simple motifs that may have one or two elements of the design missing can often be repaired at home.

1 Replacing a missing part
Clean out the recess that is left by the missing part. Tape a thin piece of paper over the design and use a soft pencil or wax crayon to make a rubbing of the recess. Using a watersoluble gum, stick the paper pattern to the selected veneer, making sure that the grain is in the right direction. Leave it to dry under a weighted block.

2 Fitting the veneer
Cut the part to shape with a knife, following the pattern. Use a metal ruler as a guide for straight cuts and cut curves freehand. Check for fit and make fine adjustments by sanding the edges. Glue it into place and either press it with a hammer or clamp it with a block until it has set. Sand the patch lightly to make it ready for finishing.

Shading veneer
Some traditional decorative motifs have parts of the assembly shaded to give a three-dimensional effect. If need be, you can reproduce a similar piece using heated sand.

Using hot sand
Fill a flat tin or foil dish with fine silver sand. Heat the sand on the stove at a low heat. Cut the veneer a little oversize and insert the appropriate edge into the hot sand. After a few seconds lift the veneer with tweezers to check the color. Repeat as required.

To test the final color, as it will appear when it is finished, lightly sand the surface and dampen it. If it is satisfactory, cut and fit the part (as above), making sure that the shaded portion is facing the correct direction.

THE FRAILTY OF OLD TEXTILES

Textiles that arecomposed of organic fibers begin to deteriorate from the moment the cloth comes off the loom. Expert conservation can slow down the process, but nothing can stop it. For this and other reasons, textiles are more vulnerable than most antiques.

Exposure to strong light causes irreversible deterioration of the fabric, resulting in faded colors and brittle fibers. Damp conditions or high levels of humidity are also very damaging, leading to mold growth and in extreme cases causing colors to run. Dry heat can be harmful, too, as it causes the fibers to become brittle. Textiles need to be protected from airborne pollution and dust, which can stain and abrade fabrics and tarnish metallic threads. Dust also attracts harmful insects to textiles, which offer a ready supply of food for their larvae.

It can be difficult—if not impossible—to restore textiles once they have been subjected to a harmful environment. It is therefore essential to store and display them carefully, in order to protect your collection from some of the more obvious risks. Textiles also suffer from careless handling —so, when you are cleaning and repairing them, remove rings or other jewelry that might become snagged in the fabric and, to avoid the possibility of staining and cigarette burns, don't drink or smoke. Even the acidic oil we all have on our fingers is harmful to antique textiles, so it is advisable to wash your hands before handling them.

TEXTILES

Even if you do not specifically collect antique textiles, you probably own and use an old tablecloth or perhaps a fireside rug or some embroidered cushion covers that have been passed down to you from your grandparents or a great-aunt. Textiles are common heirlooms—possibly because they never seem to outlive their usefulness, despite the fact that fashions change and you may no longer wear clothes that you bought just a few years ago. Nevertheless, costumes and accessories such as hats, bags, and shoes are highly collectable. So are samplers, wall hangings and painted textiles, which in some cases can be construed as works of art.

The majority of textiles are woven (that is, with the longitudinal warp threads interlaced by transverse weft threads), but there are also knitted, crocheted, knotted, and braided textiles, all of which have special qualities that appeal to collectors.

We tend to think of antique textiles as being made from natural materials, such as cotton, linen, wool, and silk—but synthetic fibers began to be used for manufacturing cloth from around the 1900s.

CLEANING TEXTILES

Cleaning not only improves the appearance of most antique textiles, it also removes soiling, which is often the catalyst for deterioration. Consequently, even very old and fragile items may need to be cleaned for their own protection, although this should only be done by experts.

Since items are often constructed from a number of different fabrics, it is important to examine them carefully before deciding on the best method of cleaning. This is not always as straightforward as it might seem, and you may have to get advice from a trained conservator.

GETTING EXPERT ADVICE

There are excellent textile restorers who work for antique dealers, but they may not have the in-depth technical background of a trained conservator. If you have an item that needs cleaning, but you are unsure of the best way to go about it, a textile conservator is probably your safest bet for reliable advice.

One way to find expert help is to call a local museum. Even if there is no conservation department on site, the museum staff are bound to hire private consultants and conservators and should be able to recommend one to you.

Alternatively, a museum may be able to put you in touch with an organization that has a list of conservators who are working in your area. You will probably be sent the names and addresses of three or four experts who are willing to offer advice or even undertake the work for you.

You should not feel any embarrassment about taking items that are not particularly valuable to a conservator. He or she will always give you a range of options, depending on what you can afford to have done. Even if that advice is to store the textile safely until you can do something more constructive, you will at least have the benefit of an informed opinion upon which to base your decision.

Testing for fugitive dyes

Probably the most important decision you will have to make is whether you can safely wash an item in water. "Wet cleaning" is an irreversible process, so you have to be sure that do you need to be sure that the piece is not going to shrink, but it is imperative that you find out whether any part of the textile is colored with a fugitive dye that is going to run when it is immersed in water. It is the safest option to assume that a dye will run until you have tested it—and that means checking every color separately, including the dyes that are used for trimmings and linings, embroidery threads, and even patches and threads that may have been used for previous restorations. If there is the slightest indication that the textile contains fibers colored with fugitive dyes, then don't wash the piece in water. Solvent cleaning is a possibility, but it should only be undertaken by a qualified conservator.

Testing individual samples

The most accurate method is to test a sample thread from every part of the piece that you want to clean. Using tweezers and sharp nail scissors, trim a ⅛ inch (3mm) length of thread from a hem, the inside of a pocket, a long tail end of an embroidery thread, or anywhere that can't be seen and where you won't damage the piece.

For the test, sandwich the sample threads between a pair of transparent glass weights. You can either buy these from a conservators' supplier, or get a glazier to cut two 4 x ½ inch (100 x 40mm) pieces of glass ⅛ inch (3mm) thick and polish off the sharp edges.

1 Mounting the samples
Place a piece of blotting paper on one of the glass weights and lay your sample threads on the paper. If you have samples of a similar color, label them for identification.

2 Wetting the samples
Make up a solution using the same proportion of soap and water as you intend to use for washing the piece. Using a dropper or an artist's paintbrush, deposit a small drop of solution onto each sample thread.

3 Applying the second weight
Put the other weight on top of the samples and monitor them for a few hours to see if any color transfers onto the blotting paper.

Testing with a cotton wool bud

Although testing individual samples is preferable, you may not be able to find a thread end that you can remove without harming the textile. Instead, barely moisten a cotton wool bud with a soap solution (see page 114) and touch it lightly against the surface of the cloth. You should only make this test on the inside of a hem or on a seam that is normally hidden—and don't attempt it on anything valuable. If you detect color on the surface of the bud or on the blotting paper that is pressed against the cloth, don't wash the item in water.

Be aware that some dyes take time before they run—which is why monitoring a variety of individual thread samples over a period of hours is a more accurate test.

Washing textiles

Even when you are confident that the color will not run, you still need to identify the fabric in order to know how it is likely to react when it is soaked in water. If you are in doubt, look for a manufacturer's label or seek expert advice.

Cotton and linen are generally safe to wash, but be wary about wetting wool. It reacts badly to hot water, and any abrasion is likely to cause "felting." Don't wash rayon or early viscose; nor put mixed-fiber textiles in water, as they are liable to differential drying and shrinkage.

It is not a good idea to wash beaded items, wall hangings or large, heavy garments; and never wash very fragile or valuable textiles yourself. Have all of these cleaned by a conservator.

Removing buttons and fastenings
Before you put textiles in water, be sure to remove any buttons or fastenings that are made with metal components and check that there are no metallic threads that have been woven into the piece that might cause rust staining. Also, remove any collectable buttons that could be harmed by immersion in water. It is worth noting that professional conservators retain the thread that is used to attach buttons or fastenings as evidence of historic construction.

Removing loose dust and grit
Before you wash anything, always vacuum it first to remove grit and harmful particles that are trapped in the weave of the textile. If you fail to remove them, the water may push these impurities deeper into the fibers.
Dust tends to collect in cuffs, hems, and pockets. Remove it with a soft brush and a vacuum-suction unit (see page 116). Check first that there are no small objects of interest that have been left in the pockets.

113

Washing clothing

As long as they are in a reasonable condition, cotton shirts and blouses, christening dresses, and white cotton underwear are the type of garments that you can usually wash safely by hand. It is possible to support holes and worn areas with a white nylon net to prevent them from fraying while the piece is washed and dried—but it is not advisable to immerse any garment that shows signs of general deterioration. Never wash old textiles in a washing machine.

Remember to vacuum the garment before you wash it. Also, make sure that you have everything you need on hand before putting the item into the water.

Mixing a soap solution

Some textiles will benefit from soaking them in water only, but ingrained soiling is likely to have been contaminated by grease particles that cannot be removed without some form of detergent. Unfortunately, the majority of modern detergents contain so many additives (bleaches, brighteners, enzymes) that they are potentially harmful to antique textiles. It is therefore the safest to only use pure soap flakes that are recommended for washing woolens. Never use perfumed or colored soaps—nor liquid dishwashing soap—to wash old textiles.

Any soap that you use has to be rinsed out, so it makes sense to use as little as possible. The ideal concentration is ¾ oz (20g) of soap flakes to 1¾ pints (1L) of water. The easiest method is to measure the amount of water you need into a bowl or bathtub, then to calculate the amount of soap you require to achieve the ideal concentration. Don't expect to generate foam—unless the water is extremely soft, foam indicates that there is too much soap in the solution.

Hot water can be very damaging, so always use lukewarm water—around 68–77°F (20–25°C). Ideally you should use soft water for washing and rinsing, changing to deionized water for the final rinse. A domestic filtration system that removes earth metals (magnesium, calcium, and aluminum) is an advantage. You could wash small items in distilled water, or boil tap water and let it cool down before you use it.

As a last resort, run water into the bathtub and leave it for around 20 minutes to allow the chlorine to evaporate. Do the same between rinses.

1 Sponging the garment
Lower the garment into the water and arrange it so that it lies as flat as possible. Leave it to soak for around ten minutes, then dab it all over with a sponge to disturb the dirt. Don't squeeze or rub the fabric vigorously. Turn it over carefully and sponge the other side.

2 Rinsing it in clean water
Pick up the garment in both hands and carefully lift it out of the dirty water. Refill the bathtub with freshwater and replace the garment, sponging it gently all over—rinse in two or three changes of water. If there are any bubbles or the fabric has an iridescent sheen, rinse it again.

As a final test, take a small sample of water from the last rinse in a glass, place your hand over the top of the glass and shake the water vigorously. If any bubbles appear, rinse the item once more, then test the water again.

3 Drying it flat
Blot the garment between dry, white towels to remove any excess water. Because heat accelerates the deterioration of antique textiles, conservators never iron old fabrics. Instead, lay the rinsed garment flat on a thick, white towel in a well-ventilated room to dry naturally or use an electric fan or a hair dryer to blow cold air across the piece while you smooth out the creases by hand.

Preserving the shape

Fabrics invariably change shape when they hold water, and they often have to be eased back into shape as they dry, particularly when a piece has to be returned to a frame. However, for most people it is difficult to remember the exact proportions of an object unless they have a template for comparison.

1 Making a tracing

Lay two layers of transparent acetate or polyester over the item that you are going to wash and trace its outline with a fiber-tip pen. The double layer is only a precaution against the point of the pen puncturing the acetate and marking the textile with ink.

2 Making a drying board

Cut out a sheet of softboard that is larger than the textile; paste a sheet of squared paper onto it to help align the grain (warp and weft) of the fabric. Place the tracing on top, then wrap the board in transparent polyethylene.

3 Drying the textile

Wash and rinse the textile, then lay it flat on the plastic-covered board to dry. The shape of the wet textile will be quite different from your tracing. As you dry the fabric with a cold hair dryer or a fan, gradually ease it back into shape, using the graph paper and tracing as a guide. Avoid stretching the fabric.

Supporting delicate textiles

Textiles are particularly vulnerable when they are wet because they can tear under their own weight. Consequently you need to support delicate textiles on a piece of fine nylon netting when washing them.

Cut the netting larger than the textile, so that you can hold it in both hands when lowering the piece into the water and when taking it out again. It is convenient to wash small items in a photographer's plastic tray.

Washing and drying delicate textiles

Wash and rinse the textile (as described opposite), supporting it on the netting (see below left) each time you lift it out to change the water. Leave the textile on its support to dry flat on a clean towel or a polyethylene-covered board. Alternatively, leave the piece to dry naturally on a drying rack that is made from soft cotton netting stretched over a frame.

Supporting weaker areas of the fabric

Before washing any piece of antique textile, examine it carefully for weak areas that may need to be supported before it is immersed in water. It helps to tack a patch of white nylon netting over holes or frayed edges—but get expert advice if the textile appears to be in very fragile condition.

REMOVING STAINS

It is natural to want to remove disfiguring stains from antique textiles—since ingrained soiling is very likely to be acidic, it is probably also advantageous in terms of conservation. Nevertheless, lifting heavy soiling is not always entirely beneficial.

The main problem is identifying the nature of a stain in order to select the appropriate solvent. If the wrong solvent is applied, it can make removal even more difficult—and many old stains prove to be permanent. Accurate identification can be tricky, even for professional restorers, so do not hesitate to seek the advice of a trained textile conservator.

Secondly, you would not want to reduce the value of a piece by removing a stain that is part of its history. For example, cleaning a soiled uniform that has been worn in a battle could eradicate all the clues about its provenance and greatly reduce its interest to collectors and historians. Some form of cleaning may be necessary if the stains are harming the uniform; but, again, it is advisable to get an informed opinion before taking action.

In short, removing old stains may do more harm than good—and it is always wisest to obtain expert advice before you proceed.

Dealing with mildew

If textiles have been stored in damp conditions, mildew staining may be evident. Wet cleaning will probably push the soiling deeper into the fibers of the textile, so your best option is to allow the fabric to dry thoroughly, then try removing the mildew with vacuum suction and a sable brush (see page 116). If that doesn't work, take the piece to a professional.

Rust stains

Rusty fastenings can stain fabrics. This is a condition that needs treatment because it will eventually weaken the textile. However, do not be tempted to bleach the fabric; take it to a conservator for a professional opinion.

See also Emergency measures (page 120).

DRY-CLEANING METHODS

The chemicals that are used by ordinary dry cleaners are not suitable for antique clothes and textiles. However, there are specialists who are able to dry-clean older pieces that cannot be washed in water. Professional textile conservators are also trained in dry-cleaning methods.

As long as the piece is not heavily soiled, you can remove a noticeable amount of dust and dirt using vacuum suction.

Vacuum cleaning

Removing dust with vacuum suction is the safest way to clean old textiles, as long as the piece is not fragile. However, most domestic vacuum cleaners are too powerful for conserving textiles, unless they are attached with a dial or switch that reduces the suction. Conservators' suppliers stock adapters that reduce the suction level of ordinary machines, and you can buy suitable battery-operated vacuum-suction units from similar sources. Even when you are using a reduced-suction vacuum cleaner, hold the nozzle a little way above the surface of the textile—never in contact with the fabric.

Cleaning embroidery
When you are extracting dust from embroidery, smocking, or any textile of a three-dimensional nature, brush it gently with an artist's sable brush while holding the nozzle of the vacuum-suction unit close to the tip of the brush.

A makeshift filter
To prevent loose threads, small fastenings, or beads from being pulled into the vacuum cleaner, stretch a piece of fine white nylon netting over the nozzle and secure it with a rubber band.

Always examine beaded textiles carefully before vacuum cleaning them, to make sure that the beads are held in place with tight threads. Use a cotton bud that has been barely moistened with distilled water to remove greasy deposits from the surface of the beads.

Cleaning metallic threads
Metallic threads used to make epaulets, frogs, and military insignia can become badly tarnished. Clean the surface with vacuum suction, then take a cotton bud that has been barely moistened with distilled water and dab the surface of the threads. The effect may not be dramatic, but if you examine the surface of the cotton bud, you will see how much dirt is being removed. Don't attempt to remove tarnish with metal polish.

MAKING MINOR REPAIRS

Repairs to valuable textiles and historical costumes should be left to a conservator, but there are many items that are sold in antique markets and secondhand-clothing stores that only need a few minor repairs to give them a new lease of life.

Don't attempt to replace worn embroidery or missing beads with modern materials. It is better to live with old textiles that are less than perfect, rather than risk reducing their value or appearance through inappropriate restoration.

Also be aware of "historical" wear. Worn cuffs and buttonholes are only to be expected in a garment that has seen fair wear and tear and detract little from its appeal. You may even find that a collar has been "turned" at some time in the past in order to prolong the useful life of a well-worn garment. That is also an interesting clue to its past history, and you would be advised to leave it alone unless the old repair is actually causing damage to the costume.

On the other hand, sewing up a loose hem or patching a torn sleeve can do little harm—and you may end up tearing the garment if you don't make repairs of this type at the earliest opportunity.

An approach to repairing textiles

Before deciding what to do with a damaged textile, try to determine what is likely to be the future role of the piece in question.

If it is to be mounted only for display, you might choose to do little more than slow down the present deterioration. If, on the other hand, you intend to use or wear a particular item, then you will probably want to undertake repairs that allow the piece to function reasonably well, while at the same time protecting it from unnecessary damage. For example, you would most likely want to replace broken or missing fastenings before wearing an article of period clothing—and it is worth patching a small hole in a tablecloth before someone accidentally converts the hole into a tear.

Any textile in fragile condition should be examined by an expert before you attempt to even make small repairs. Weak textiles may require full support before they can be displayed, and that is a job that is best left to a professional who can ensure that the weight of the textile is held by the support, and not the other way around.

There are few strict rules to guide you—except that any repair should be reversible (so never use adhesives to mend antique textiles), and if you need to repair something you deeply care about, have it restored by a conservator unless you have complete confidence in your own ability.

Choosing sympathetic materials

Any expert will tell you that if you are going to repair old textiles, you should always use materials that are sympathetic to the item that you are restoring. However, that advice can be interpreted in different ways.

One school of thought says that you should always choose similar materials—so that, by using identical materials, you ensure that the old and the new will react in harmony and age at a similar rate. However, common sense tells you that there may be little point in repairing a silk textile with a comparatively weak silk thread, when a stranded embroidery thread would make a repair last longer and therefore save the textile from unnecessary handling and stress in the future.

In order to achieve sympathetic repairs, try to find fabrics that are identical in color and similar to the original article in weight and density of the weave.

Needles

When you are making stitched repairs, it is important to select an appropriate needle for the fabric that you are restoring. Perhaps the most vital factor is size. If, for example, you are sewing a fine silk or a cotton lawn, choose a very fine needle to avoid leaving holes in the fabric. Embroidery needles are ideal because they have very sharp points. Some conservators like to use exceptionally fine beading needles when they are repairing delicate fabrics. Discard blunt needles, which will damage the weave.

Curved needles are often required for mounting textiles on a fabric-covered board. If you can't find one the right size, improvise by bending a straight needle.

Fine sewing threads

When you are patching very fine fabrics, it can be problematic to find equally fine sewing threads that are strong enough. You might try using cotton lace-making yarn, which you can buy from most haberdashers (fabric stores). You could also use crewel wool, polyester, silk, or mercerized-cotton threads. Some conservators go to the trouble of pulling a thread out of a piece of finely woven polyester fabric; the pulled thread is as fine as a human hair, and practically invisible when it is stitched into a repair.

PATCHING UP DAMAGED TEXTILES

Never sew up the edges of a torn textile, nor darn any holes. The stitching will inevitably put strain on the surrounding fabric and will probably make the damage even worse. Always patch both tears and holes to support the weakened fabric, especially if the item is to be worn or hung. However, the tension must be exactly right if the patch is not going to cause further damage—a badly applied patch is likely to cause more problems than it solves.

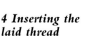

Mending torn fabric

Although patches are always applied to the back of the textile, you should work from the front, with your support stitches visible on the face of the textile. This is why the sewing thread must be as fine as is practicable and also a good color match. Working from the front allows you to see exactly what you are doing and lets you monitor the progress of the repair.

Since it is particularly difficult to patch three-dimensional textiles, such as puffed sleeves or bonnets, take these to an expert for repair.

1 Cutting out the patch
Select an appropriate support fabric for the repair and cut out a patch, using pinking shears. Make the patch large enough to ensure that the edges can be sewn into the stronger areas of the textile—not just into the relatively weak fabric around the tear itself.

2 Arranging the torn edges
Before you apply the patch, arrange the torn fabric so that the warp and weft threads are aligned correctly and are as straight as possible. Allow the torn edges to butt up against each other but not to overlap. Smooth down any frayed edges so that the cloth is lying flat.

3 Pinning the patch into place
Pin the patch to the back of the textile, using fine straight pins. Check that the torn edges are still butted together neatly.

4 Inserting the laid thread
Torn fabric is repaired with laid couching stitches, applied at a 90 degree angle to the tear and running from one strong area of the fabric to the other.

To make the first laid thread, bring your threaded needle up on one side, then take the thread in a straight line across the tear and down through the fabric again.

5 Couching the thread

Bring the needle back up next to the laid thread, around ⅛ inch (3mm) from where it last entered the fabric. Take the needle over the laid thread and back through the fabric to form a small couching stitch that anchors the laid thread in place.

6 Completing a row of couching stitches

Continue to make similar couching stitches at ⅛ inch (3mm) intervals along the laid thread.

7 Continuing with support stitches

Insert a second laid thread about ⅛ inch (3mm) to one side, parallel to the one you have just couched, and anchor it with couching stitches. Continue with laid couching stitches along the entire length of the tear.

8 Sewing the edges of the patch

If the patch is larger than around 2½ inches (65mm) square, secure its edges to the textile with herringbone stitches. There is no need to sew the edges of smaller patches.

Patching up a hole

Proceed with patching a hole, using the method described for repairing torn cloth, but use staggered long-and-short stitches to secure the edges

REPLACING BUTTONS AND FASTENINGS

Although it may be difficult to find an exact replacement for a single missing button or fastening, it is relatively easy to track down a set of genuine period buttons to complement, for example, a Victorian dress or a 1930s overcoat. Antique buttons are collector's items, so check their value or rarity before wearing them. Don't cut buttons off an original show card, since that is collectable too.

Securing loose beads

Examine antique beads carefully to see if any of the threads that hold the beads in place have broken.

Sewing individual beads

If possible, figure out the type of stitching that was originally used and copy it when you are securing loose beads. If you are in doubt, cast on the thread as close to the bead as possible, secure the bead with two stitches, and then cast off the thread, leaving a long thread end.

Securing a row of beads

Often beads were threaded onto a single thread that was then sewn onto the backing fabric. As a result, if one bead comes loose, you could lose the entire row. To prevent that from happening, secure the row of beads with couching stitches and sew over the loose thread end to anchor it to the fabric.

USING AND STORING TEXTILES

The majority of items in most antique textile collections are rarely put out on display, usually because they don't allow for convenient presentation. But there are exceptions, such as wall hangings, samplers, and other embroideries—all of which have similarities to pictures and other two-dimensional works of art. Decorated pincushions, fabric-covered shoes, or beaded purses can be stored in glass-fronted display cases, but few collectors have the space to exhibit items such as period costumes; therefore most are primarily concerned with how to keep their collections safe from deterioration. Also, when clothing, tablecloths, and other collectable items are put to use, accessible storage tends to take priority over display.

Wearing antique clothing

Fashion revivals fuel a brisk trade in old clothes that suddenly become wearable again; and heirlooms such as wedding dresses and christening gowns are often handed down to be worn by succeeding generations. There's an obvious risk of accidental damage when you wear period clothing—so inspect each piece carefully and, even more importantly, have it cleaned before putting it back into storage. Simple cotton or linen garments can be washed by hand (see page 114), but it's best to have more complex items cleaned by specialist dry cleaners. Although it is relatively expensive compared with ordinary dry cleaners, they have experience of handling delicate textiles.

Emergency measures

No matter how careful you are, there is always the possibility of spilling something that will stain clothing or domestic linen. Although most stained items should be taken to a specialist cleaner as soon as possible, it pays to apply emergency measures to minimize the damage.

There is no guarantee that they will work—but, since the damage is already done, there is little to lose.

• Red wine
To neutralize the effect of spilling red wine, immediately pour white wine onto the stain. Alternatively, if you have washed the piece successfully in the past, leave it to soak in cold water.

For textiles that cannot be wet-cleaned, pour a large amount of salt onto the stain and leave it to absorb the wine. The next day remove the salt with vacuum suction.

• Strawberry or raspberry jam
If you know that a tablecloth is safe to wash, soak jam stains in very hot water.

• Candle wax
If candle wax drips onto a tablecloth or napkins, pick off the hardened lumps, then cover the stain with brown packing paper, with the shiny side up. Press the paper with a warm domestic iron to melt the wax and pull it out of the fabric. Repeat the process with clean paper until all the wax is removed.

• Perspiration stains
Perspiration stains are virtually impossible to remove, especially from silk and synthetic fibers. Specialist dry-cleaning with solvents may have an effect—but the chances are slim.

• Ink
Blot up as much of the ink as possible and take the damaged item to a textile conservator without delay.

• Mud
Let mud dry, then gently brush it off while using vacuum suction (see page 116). Never attempt to remove mud while it is still wet.

• Saturation
A burst pipe or a flood is potentially disastrous for antique textiles. If you allow them to dry out, any water staining may become permanent. Wrap saturated textiles in polyethylene and put them into a freezer, then take them to a conservator as soon as possible.

Storing textiles

Antique textiles should be stored in the dark to protect them from the effects of ultraviolet light. A dry, cool environment is also essential.

Wrapping them in tissue paper

Ideally textiles should be wrapped in acid-free tissue paper and stored flat in strong acid-free cardboard boxes. If you have to fold textiles for storage, pad each fold with a roll of tissue paper to prevent it from becoming a permanent crease.

Storing flat textiles on tubes

Roll larger pieces, face side out, on an acid-free cardboard tube or plastic drainage pipes that have been covered with tissue paper. Make sure that the grain is straight and, if possible, roll the textile in the direction of the warps.

Lay more sheets of paper on top of the textile as you begin to roll it onto the tube. Secure the roll with white cotton tape or, even better, wrap it in a sheet of washed calico.

Storing clothing

You can store old clothes in acid-free cardboard boxes (as described above), but make sure that you pad sleeves, bodices, and folds with tissue paper.

To prevent metal buttons from staining the fabric, cut "button holes" in small squares of acid-free tissue paper and slip them over the buttons.

Nothing you do will prevent silver buttons from tarnishing if they are sewn onto a woolen garment. Metallic threadwork that is found on military uniforms may be affected similarly and, although a conservator can clean it for you, the metal will tarnish again after a relatively short period.

Before putting items of clothing into storage, remove any pins or brooches that are attached to them.

Storing accessories

Pad hats and shoes with acid-free tissue paper to help them keep their shape. Store them in cardboard archival boxes with metal-reinforced corners. Protect evening bags and purses in a similar way, making sure that they are not piled on top of each other in storage.

Hanging garments

Hang larger garments from padded coat hangers and cover them with calico bags, that are tied at the bottom with tape. Don't use plastic bags—they attract dust and encourage mold growth.

Padding a coat hanger
Choose a strong coat hanger, preferably one that has a straight trouser rail and which fits the shoulder width of the garment you are storing.

Wrap the coat hanger in polyester wadding—the type that is used for making quilts—that is available from any department store. Ensure that the padding is adequate for the shoulders and to support the upper part of the garment, if need be adding a second layer of wadding. Stitch through the wadding with white cotton thread to hold it in place, then cover it with washed calico.

If it is required, you can extend the wadding below the coat hanger and shape it with scissors to pad out the bodice of a dress.

Sewing loops to a waistband
In order to suspend a skirt from a coat hanger, sew wide cotton tape loops to the waistband—one on the front, one on the back, and one on each side.

Hang a heavy beaded dress—or dresses that are delicate or weak—from similar tapes that take the strain off the bodice. Run the tapes up from the waistband to support the weight of the skirt on the coat hanger.

PROTECTING TEXTILES FROM MOTHS

Moths sometimes lay their eggs on silk, but they are particularly attracted to the sulfur that is present in wool. When the larvae hatch, they feed on the fibers of the textile, leaving the characteristic ragged holes.

To protect your collection from infestations, make sure that the textiles themselves are clean before you store them, and dust or vacuum the insides of cupboards, drawers and wardrobes.

Rub cedar oil into the inside of wooden drawers and wardrobes (you can get it from anywhere that sells aromatherapy oils). Cedar oil not only keeps moths at bay but fills the space with an attractive scent.

No textile conservator would ever advocate the use of mothballs—naphthalene can be a health risk under certain circumstances.

Eradicating moths

If you discover live moths in your wardrobe or detect signs of an infestation, wrap all the stored textiles in plastic bags and take them outside where you can brush and vacuum them to remove any remaining insect eggs. Make sure that you vacuum seams, pockets, and cuffs thoroughly. As a precaution, clean all the garments in the wardrobe and consider having them fumigated by an expert.

Freezing is a definite way of eradicating an infestation, but you need to wrap the textiles in polyethylene and leave them for a week in a freezer that can be set to a temperature of 4°F. Unless you have access to an industrial freezer, ask the conservation department at a local museum to recommend someone who has a suitable facility. Vacuum the textiles after they have thawed out.

DISPLAYING TEXTILES

Antique textiles make delightful wall hangings, but they need to be mounted and displayed carefully in order to protect them from damage. Museums display textiles in low levels of lighting that are impractical at home, but since you need to protect your collection from damaging levels of ultraviolet light, never hang textiles in direct sunlight or illuminate them with spotlights. Net curtains or half-drawn blinds help reduce daylight to an acceptable level, and it is worth drawing the curtains in rooms that are not used during the day.

Textiles will be harmed if you hang them above a source of heat, such as a radiator or an open fire. Warm, rising air makes fibers brittle and deposits dust onto unprotected textiles.

Don't hang textiles on outside walls that suffer from penetrating moisture or condensation.

Like drawings and prints, antique textiles should ideally be mounted behind glass—but if you have a wall hanging that is too large for framing, suspend it from a batten to distribute the weight evenly, thus reducing the strain on the weaker areas of the textile.

Framing textiles

Small embroidered samplers and delicate pieces of lace can be framed like pictures, but it is worth discussing your plans with a conservator in case there is something about your item that is unusual or might prove to be difficult to handle.

Amateurs can safely mount textiles that are around the size of a man's handkerchief. Anything larger, especially if it is fragile, is best left to a professional who has done this type of work before.

Choosing a frame

Don't use ready-made picture frames for displaying antique textiles. Since the piece is to be sealed behind glass, it is imperative that all the materials that are used to construct the frame are inert, otherwise they may harm the textile over a period of time. An experienced framer or a textile conservator will advise you to stay away from frames that are made from pine, oak, or mahogany. You should also seal the inner face of the frame's backing board to prevent acids from leaching into the fibers of the textile. Professionals tend to use an iron-on foil sheet, which you can buy from a conservators' supplier.

The surface of the textile should not be allowed to touch the glass—so make sure that the rabbet in the frame is deep enough for a narrow fillet, or use a thick window mount cut from acid-free cardboard (see pages 24–25).

Mounting textiles

Before they are framed, antique textiles should be supported on a padded board. Make the mounting board from acid-free cardboard and cotton domette, covered with a fabric—linen or cotton is a good choice—that compliments the antique textile. Wash the covering fabric in hot water, without adding detergent, to ensure that it is preshrunk before being mounted and to remove the manufacturer's dressing. Dry and iron the fabric. Similarly, wash the cotton domette in warm water.

1 Making the mounting board

To make a mounting board that will stay flat, glue together two sheets of acid-free cardboard, with the grain of each board running at 90 degree angle to the other. Use water-based PVA adhesive. Cut the finished board at least ¾ inches (18mm) larger all around than the textile that is to be mounted, in order to create a handling edge.

2 Padding the mounting board

Cut a piece of cotton domette about three inches (75mm) larger all around than the mounting board. Place the board in the center of the domette so that it aligns accurately with the warp and weft threads. Holding the board down firmly with one hand, fold the edges of the fabric over and secure them with glass-headed pins that are driven into the edges of the cardboard.

3 Adjusting the tension

To check that the tension is adequate, lay the padded board face up on a work surface and run the tip of your finger firmly along the center of the board. If the domette ripples, take in the excess by removing the pins and putting a little more tension on the fabric. If the board buckles, release the tension on the domette. Adjust the tension across the width of the board in the same way.

4 Gluing the domette

Lay the board face down again and paint a strip of PVA adhesive around the perimeter of the card. Fold the edges of the domette over and rub them down onto the glue, cutting miters at each corner so that the fabric will lie flat. Let the glue set and remove the pins.

5 Mounting the covering fabric

Cut out a piece of fabric one to two inches (25–50mm) larger all around than the domette. Stretch it over the padded board (see left), then check that the tension is adequate and glue the fabric onto the back of the board. Make sure that the warp and weft threads are parallel with the edges of the cardboard, then cut miters at each corner. Leave the glue to set.

6 Aligning the textile

It helps to set up a temporary guide for mounting the textile sample onto the board. This is especially useful when you are mounting asymmetrical samples. Insert pins into the edges of the board, equidistant from each corner. Lightly stretch the cotton threads from pin to pin across the board.

7 Pinning the textile into place

Having carried out any repairs that are required to conserve the textile, lay it centrally onto the fabric-covered board and pin it into place with a straight, glass-headed pin driven through each corner into the cardboard. Add other pins as needed to pull the textile firmly, but don't stretch it. Make sure that the grain of the textile aligns with that of the covering fabric.

8 Stitching the textile to the fabric

Using a fine curved needle, sew the textile to the backing fabric with herringbone stitches. Sew across the top edge, down the sides, then across the bottom, gradually removing the pins as the work progresses.

Cast off with two small stitches, pass the needle back through the line of herringbone stitches for about one inch (25mm), then cut off the thread.

Finally, mount the textile in the frame and tape the back to seal out any dust (see pages 24–25).

Hanging larger textiles

To display textiles that are too large to mount behind glass, attach them to a linen or cotton-downproof lining and suspend the lining from a wall-hung batten. Wash the lining to remove the manufacturer's dressing. Then dry and iron it flat, ensuring that the grain of the fabric is not distorted.

Get a professional to line any textile that is larger than one square yard (1m²).

Attaching the lining

On all sides the finished lining should be ¼ inch (6mm) smaller than the textile. When you are measuring the fabric for the lining, include an extra ⅜ inch (10mm) for every one foot (300mm) across the width and from the top to the bottom. This excess fabric will ensure that the textile will not buckle if the lining contracts for any reason. In addition, allow for a 1¼ inches (30mm) fold on all four edges of the lining.

Pinning the lining to the textile
Lay the textile face down, aligned with the front edge of the work surface. Fold the edges of the lining fabric under and pin it to the textile—each folded edge should be ¼ inch (6mm) from the edge of the textile. Use glass-headed pins that are spaced 1½ inches (40mm) apart. As you pin the lining in place, gradually take in the excess fabric.

Using a lining stitch

A lining stitch holds the lining close to the textile, preventing the progress of insects and dust particles.

1 Inserting the needle into the folded edge
To make each stitch, insert the needle into the folded edge of the lining and let the point emerge ⅜ inch (10mm) farther along. Pass the needle down through the textile beside the hole from which the thread emerges from the folded edge of the lining.

2 Backstitching
Pass the needle back up through the textile 1/32 inch (1mm) to the right, then insert the point of the needle into the same hole in the folded edge of the lining.

3 Putting tension on the stitch
Let the point of the needle emerge ⅜ inch (10mm) farther along the folded edge, then pull on the thread to bring the lining close to the textile. Make a similar lining stitch at that point.

Using hook-and-loop tape

Having stitched the lining to the textile on all four sides, attach the hanging to a wall-hung batten using peel-off Velcro hook-and-loop tape.

1 Sewing the tape to the hanging
Using a relatively thick polyester thread, sew the softer half of the tape along the top edge of the lining. Use V-shaped stitches, around ¼ inch (6mm) long, that pass right through the lining and the textile. Don't machine-stitch the tape to the hanging.

2 Stapling the tape to the batten
Screw the batten into the wall and attach the other half of the tape to the batten with strong upholsterer's staples.

3 Mounting the hanging to the batten
Get someone to help you mount the hanging onto the batten. One method is to roll the hanging and begin attaching it at one end of the batten. Press the two halves of the Velcro tape together, while your assistant supports the weight of the hanging and unrolls it as you proceed.

Alternatively, mark the center of the batten, place the midpoint of the hanging on that mark, and work outward from the center. You may need two assistants for this method.

Once the hanging is attached to the batten, you can make any minor adjustments necessary.

RUGS AND CARPETS

Many machine-made rugs and carpets are attractive as well as durable, but collectors are almost invariably drawn to handwoven or knotted-pile rugs. Though it is a rather specialized form of textile, all rugs are basically warp-and-weft based. In terms of manufacturing the flat-woven kilims and sumaks are hardly distinguishable from other woven textiles, but knotted-pile rugs and carpets are made in a very different way.

Making knotted-pile rugs

Wool or sometimes silk yarn is tied into a knot around pairs of parallel warp threads that run from the top of the loom to the bottom. Having completed a row of knots, the weaver introduces transverse weft threads that are beaten down with a comb to hold the knots securely to the foundation threads. After each knot is tied, the yarn is severed with a knife; and when the row is complete, the knot ends are trimmed to the correct length with scissors, forming a short, tufted pile.

As the work progresses, the weaver introduces yarns of various colors to create the pattern of the rug. Being handmade—often by nomadic peoples who have to dismantle the loom frequently—the pattern of oriental rugs is rarely regular or symmetrical and the color of the yarns can vary considerably—but far from detracting from their value, it is these variations that give antique rugs their special appeal and charm.

A comparatively narrow, flat-woven strip at each end of the rug protects the knotted pile and, along with the fringe, forms a decorative border. The fringes are made from the warp threads that have been cut from the loom and are sometimes knotted to form long tassels.

TYPES OF KNOTS

The type of knots that are used to make rugs varies according to local traditions. The two most common types are the Turkish or Ghiordes knot and the asymmetric Persian or Senneh knot. The Turkish Jufti knot is similar to the Ghiordes knot, but it is tied around four foundation warps instead of the usual two.

Because of the movement of various tribes and peoples in the past, it is impossible to be absolutely certain about where these different knots were used, but on the whole the Ghiordes knot derives from Turkey and from parts of western Iran and the Caucasus. The Persian Senneh knot is found in rugs made in Iran, India, and China.

TURKISH OR GHIORDES KNOT   PERSIAN OR SENNEH KNOT

JUFTI KNOT

CLEANING RUGS AND CARPETS

Rugs and carpets need regular cleaning to prevent infestations of moths and carpet beetles, and to remove minute particles of grit that wear away at the fibers. Although vacuum suction is the norm for cleaning modern floor coverings, it is unwise to use an ordinary domestic vacuum cleaner on antique rugs and carpets, especially if they are in a fragile condition—since, as soon as a rug begins to wear, powerful suction can pull it apart. Unless you are prepared to invest in a museum-quality low-suction vacuum cleaner, it is much safer to remove dust and dirt from knotted carpets and kilims with a soft-bristle brush. This is also the method that is recommended for cleaning any silk rug.

Try to brush your floor coverings once a week, and consult an oriental-rug specialist about the advisability of having them cleaned every couple of years. Once a month lift a rug or carpet so that you can sweep up the dirt from the floor beneath it and brush the back of the carpet.

Brushing carpets
Use a soft-bristle banister brush to clean antique carpets and rugs. Brush them gently by hand, only in the direction of the pile (from the top to the bottom).

Removing stains
Most people are prepared to live with a few minor stains, as long as they are not too disfiguring. In any case, stains hardly show on colorful patterned rugs and carpets. However, it pays to have an expert identify an old stain for you, in case it is doing irreparable harm to the fibers of the rug. He or she will tell you whether it's worth removing and give you an estimate for doing the work. (See also pages 128–129.)

DETECTING THE DIRECTION OF THE PILE

If you run your hand up and down the carpet, you'll find that it feels smoother in one direction and rougher in the other. When you are brushing the carpet, work in the direction that feels the smoothest. This avoids lifting the pile.

REPAIRING RUGS AND CARPETS

Nobody expects a rug that has been subjected to heavy foot traffic over the years to still be in perfect condition. Consequently, even very worn rugs may not require restoration unless they are in danger of serious deterioration.

Professional restorers perform minor miracles, including invisibly mending holes and worn-out patches. However, repairs of this type demand skill and a practiced eye able to match existing colors and recreate missing patterns. A restorer can also replace missing fringes and rebuild damaged side cords—work that is rough on the fingers and likely to damage the rug unless it is undertaken by an expert.

Nevertheless, you can avoid further deterioration by stopping your rug from fraying and by making minor repairs before the damage becomes too severe.

Preventing a rug from fraying

The kilim end—the narrow band of closely woven threads at each end of a piled rug—holds the knotted pile in place and prevents the rug from unraveling. Once a kilim end begins to fray, prompt treatment is required to protect the main patterned area of the rug from damage.

Buy a strip of upholsterer's webbing tape made from unbleached cotton. They are available up to two inches (50mm) wide, so choose one that suits the width of the kilim ends. Most department stores stock this type of tape, or you may be able to get it from a good haberdashers.

If you need to match the color of the kilim end, you can dye the tape with a cold-water dye.

Attaching the tape
Sew the tape by hand to the kilim end, following the shape of the worn-out edge. Make V-shaped stitches along both sides of the tape, using a relatively thick polyester thread. If the tape is slightly wider than you need, restrict both rows of stitches to the kilim end—don't sew the tape to the knotted pile.

Repairing worn side cords
As part of the weaving process, weft threads are wound around the last few warp threads on each side of the carpet. When the rug is finished, the edges are bound with yarn to make strong side cords. Some carpets have double side cords that are made with figure-eight binding.

Since they are thicker than the rest of the rug, the side cords wear relatively quickly. It is a good idea to replace damaged binding before the warp and weft threads begin to wear out.

1 Inserting new binding thread
Insert a threaded needle under the existing binding, right where the damage begins. Let the point emerge around ½ inch (12mm) farther along the cord.

2 Binding the edge
Working back from that point, sew over the damaged cord with neat tightly-packed stitches, —but don't pull the stitches too tight, or you will distort the line of the cord.

3 Tying off
Continue sewing ½ inch (12mm) beyond the worn-out section, then run the needle back through the new binding for around one inch (25mm) and cut off the yarn where it emerges.

USING AND DISPLAYING RUGS

Perhaps more so than most other antiques, rugs and carpets are used for their original purpose. This makes them particularly vulnerable, since floor coverings can deteriorate rapidly unless care is taken to reduce their exposure to wear and to prevent accidents from happening.

Protecting rugs from damage
Avoid using old rugs and carpets in hallways, stairs, or landings and in other areas through which there is constant traffic. The dining room is one of the worst locations for floor coverings. They not only have to bear the weight of the dining table but also scuffing from feet and chair legs is concentrated in a small area, and food and drink inevitably get spilled onto the floor. Even if you keep your antique rugs in bedrooms—where you are less likely to wear heavy shoes or boots—it pays to turn your rugs regularly to alleviate uneven wear and fading.

Don't place heavy furniture on an antique carpet. It is also advisable to use plastic furniture feet, to protect carpets from chair legs and castors.

Don't place a rug or carpet directly onto a stone, tiled, or concrete floor, or over floorboards with wide gaps between them. A good-quality underlay will reduce wear and prevents dust from blowing in between the boards, leaving dirty streaks on the surface of the floor covering. A rug that is laid over a fitted carpet requires a double-sided underlay to prevent it from moving on the pile below.

Plumbing leaks can be extremely damaging, especially those from central-heating systems that contain chemical descalers and corrosion inhibitors. Check your radiator valves regularly for leaks. Use an efficient fire screen to protect fireside rugs from sparks and falling coals.

RUGS AS WALL HANGINGS

Better-quality rugs (and ones that are too worn out to be laid on the floor) can be used as wall hangings. However, they must be hung in such a way that their weight is distributed evenly, to avoid putting any strain on weak areas. Don't hang rugs in direct sunlight, on damp walls, or over a fireplace or radiator.

Hanging a rug on a curtain rod
Make a sleeve from which to suspend the rug by stitching carpet-binding tape two inches (50mm) wide to the back of the rug, around ¾ inch (18mm) below the fringe or kilim end. Using strong polyester thread, sew along the top and bottom edges of the tape, allowing sufficient slack for the pole to pass though the sleeve.

Support each end of the rod on a wall bracket or hang the rod from chains.

Using hook-and-loop Velcro tape
Use Velcro tape to support a heavy rug. Sew one half of the tape to the back of the rug, and staple the other half to a wall-hung batten (see page 124).

Emergency measures

If an antique rug is laid on the floor, you can be sure that someone will spill something on it eventually. It is a risk we all take, but you may be able to prevent permanent staining if you act quickly. If emergency measures are unsuccessful, take the rug to a specialist for an experts opinion.

Mopping up spilled liquids
It is imperative that you mop up spilled liquids immediately, to prevent them from soaking deeply into rugs and carpets.

1 Using absorbent towels
Fold a dry white tea towel into a pad, lay it over the wet patch, and apply firm pressure. Once the cloth is thoroughly wet, apply another dry cloth and apply pressure again. Continue in this way until all the excess liquid appears to have been absorbed.

2 Drying the rug
If it is clean water that has been spilled, once you have mopped up the excess water, dry the carpet with either a hair dryer on a cold setting or an electric fan. Try raising the wet section of the carpet in order to create better circulation. When the carpet is dry, fluff up the pile with your fingertips.

Absorbing red wine

Remove as much wine as possible with absorbent towels, then sprinkle a large heap of salt onto the patch. The following morning remove the salt.

Animal urine

Urine contains acid that is injurious to textiles. It may be tempting to wash the urine out with water, but washing may make it worse.

Pick up a soiled rug immediately and either take it into the kitchen or put a sheet of plastic under the rug to protect the floor or floor covering underneath.

Mop up as much liquid as possible with clean cotton rags, then take the rug to a conservator.

As a precaution, don't place antique rugs or carpets in rooms where pets are allowed.

Removing mud

If someone treads mud across a carpet or rug, allow it to dry thoroughly, then pick off as many lumps as possible before brushing off the remaining mud.

Removing chewing gum

To remove chewing gum that has been dropped on your carpet, put an ice cube in a plastic bag and hold it against the gum. When the gum has frozen hard, carefully pick it off with a blunt kitchen knife. However, if the carpet is valuable or particularly fragile, take it to a professional—don't try to treat it yourself.

STORING RUGS AND CARPETS

Leaving a rug folded up for a long time will result in creases becoming permanent. If you have to put a rug into storage, roll it up on a piece of large-diameter plastic pipe. Choose a tube that will project from each end of the rug.

To avoid crushing the pile, always roll a knotted rug from the top. Run the palm of your hand back and forth along the rug—when the pile feels rough, your hand is moving toward the top of the rug.

Rolling a rug
Lay the rug face down and cover it with acid-free tissue paper. Place the tube at the top of the rug and roll it up, smoothing down the pile as you go. Wrap the rolled rug up in an old cotton sheet or a piece of washed calico and secure it with wide cotton tape. If it is possible, support the ends of the tube to keep the rolled rug horizontal and off the ground—don't store rolled rugs standing up.

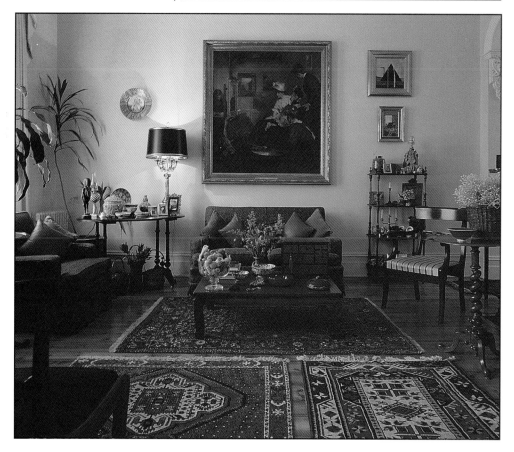

Using antique rugs as floor coverings
Use good-quality underlay when you lay antique rugs down over floorboards and protect the pile by putting protective furniture feet under the legs of a coffee table.

THE RAW MATERIALS

Plastic materials are those that at some stage of their manufacturing are malleable and capable of being molded. Although this broadly includes inorganic materials such as mortar or plaster, the term "plastics" is generally used to describe natural and synthetic materials that have a polymeric structure. Polymers are large, long-chain molecules that are made up from many (in Greek, "poly") parts.

Tortoiseshell and horn are naturally occurring organic plastic materials that can be molded with heat and pressure. Early man-made plastics were produced by processing natural substances such as rubber, cellulose, tree resins, shellac, and milk. Most plastics today, however, are based on synthetic polymers, typically derived from petrochemicals. They form an extensive range of materials with distinctive properties that vary according to their individual composition and processing.

Plastics are broadly grouped into two categories, thermoplastics and thermosetting plastics (sometimes called thermosets). Thermoplastics can be returned to their fluid state with the application of heat. In contrast, thermosetting plastics are transformed by a chemical reaction when they are cured and cannot be reversed; the majority of them are also hard and brittle, unlike the wider range of thermoplastics.

PLASTICS

We live in an age of plastics, where we are constantly in contact with plastics in one form or another. Probably more so than any other material, they have helped generate the "throw-away society"—since plastic products have become so familiar and inexpensive that we think nothing of disposing of them.

Plastic materials that are based on organic substances were developed in the mid-nineteenth century. This early pioneering work led to the birth of a new industry that developed rapidly in the 1930s with the introduction of new synthetic materials—a situation that continues to this day. Plastics were first developed as a substitute for natural materials, such as ivory, amber, and tortoiseshell, but their versatility is such that they were soon used for products that had previously been made from ceramics, wood, metal, glass, and even leather and cloth.

There is now a growing interest in old items made from plastics. However, despite modern claims that they are indestructible, all plastics will degrade eventually. The chemical nature of plastics makes them susceptible to changes in the environment, and only time will tell which plastics are the most durable. The information here briefly describes the most common plastics that were used to produce all types of products up to the 1950s and gives basic information on how to care for them.

TYPES OF PLASTICS

A collector of plastic artifacts may choose to concentrate on a particular type of material or build up a collection that is based on objects that have other merits, such as subject matter, appearance, or function. Whatever the focus of the collection is, it is helpful to know the type of plastic that is used—not just for academic reasons, but also to establish the best means of conserving the material.

The services of a laboratory would be needed to determine the precise formulation of a particular type of plastic from the range of polymers and additives that make up the different plastics used commercially. However, that is rarely necessary, and many of the clues that help to broadly identify a type of plastic can be figured out by observation based on the surface texture, color, opacity, hardness or softness, and smell. The period style and function of the object and the method of manufacturing are also useful clues. If you are in doubt, take it to a specialist dealer or a relevant museum.

METHODS OF MANUFACTURING

Most plastic materials are liquefied and formed in a mold by the application of heat and pressure, although some are produced by cold casting.

Thermoplastics that are produced as a sheet or a rod can be readily bent or pressed into shape when they are reheated. Postforming, as the method is known, was often used for early products that were made from cellulose-nitrate sheet and postwar products that were made from acrylic sheet.

Early blow-molding techniques used air to form hollow moldings, by inflating two sheets of thermoplastic material softened by heat and clamped between hollow molds. Today the method uses extruded tube, which is clamped and blown in a mold in a similar way.

Hollow moldings may also be produced by coating a heated mold with a polymer paste. This latter method, known as slush molding, is used for making flexible dolls and low-cost squeaky toys.

Extruded thermoplastics are produced by forcing the heated raw material through a shaped die and then cooling it. This method is used for making continuous lengths of a specific item.

Compression molding uses powdered thermosetting material to fill the mould—which is then heated until the plastic flows, then the mold is fully compressed. When it is cured, the mold is opened, and the plastic molding is removed.

Injection molding usually uses granules of thermoplastic material fed by a hopper into a heated chamber; when it is molten, the plastic is injected under pressure into a sealed mold.

Lines that are left in the surface of the plastic often distinguish molded objects from ones that have been fabricated by a machine—the lines indicate where the mold was split in order to remove the finished item. With injection molding, there is also a circular mark where the plastic was introduced into the mold.

Shellac

It is more commonly known as a finish for fine furniture, but shellac was also used—with the addition of organic fillers, such as wood flour, or powdered minerals, such as slate dust—to make a compression-moldable thermoplastic. The material was capable of being molded with fine detail and made into items such as boxes and photo frames. Perhaps the most common example is the 78 rpm gramophone record.

This type of plastic is a relatively brittle material and will distort if it is subjected to excessive heat. Melted shellac has the smell of sealing wax. When shellac records were superseded by ones made out of vinyl, some of the old records were handcrafted into decorative bowls or pots by softening them in hot water.

To clean shellac plastics, remove any surface dust with a soft brush and wipe with a soft cloth that has been dampened with a warm, mild liquid-soap solution.

Hard rubber

Ebonite, or vulcanite as it is also known, is a hard rubber material that came into existence around 1839, although it was not commercially produced until the middle of the nineteenth century. Originally it was made by vulcanizing natural rubber, but it was also produced using synthetic rubber when this became available in the 1940s.

Molded into a variety of small objects, including buttons, combs, jewelry, and fountain pens, ebonite typically was black —but it was also produced in a pink color for making dentures, as well as brown and a striated mixture of black and red.

Ebonite is susceptible to light and heat, which causes the surface to oxidize and take on a dull greenish-brown hue. If after handling the material, your fingers have a sulfurous odor, it indicates that the object is made from a hard rubber compound. When ebonite degrades, sulfuric acid is released and, if the plastic is wet, it can form marks known as "water spotting." Always wear cotton gloves when you are handling old pieces, to avoid moist hands transferring sulfuric-acid contaminants from one piece to another, leaving fingerprints. Handle the material as little as possible.

Maintaining ebonite
Keep vulcanized-rubber items in low light and in cool, dry conditions. Clean the surface with a soft cloth that has been dampened with a light mineral oil or apply a thin covering of microcrystalline wax. Buff with a clean, soft cloth.

Cellulose nitrate

Cellulose nitrate was developed in the mid-nineteenth century as collodion for coating photographic plates and as a treatment for wounds. From this it was developed into a plastic material (called Parkesine) by Alexander Parkes and was first shown at the International Exhibition in 1862. It was later developed in America as celluloid and in Great Britain as Xylonite. It is an important material, since cellulose nitrate was the first synthetic plastic to be manufactured from natural polymers. A variety of domestic items and playthings, as well as early cinema film, were made from it. Many of these products were postformed or blow-molded from precut sheet material that was made in a wide range of colors. Initially celluloid was produced to imitate ivory and tortoiseshell. When it is warmed, you can detect a cellulose-nitrate plastic by the distinct smell of camphor, which was used as a plasticizer during its manufacturing.

Maintaining celluloid
Celluloid is highly flammable and should not be exposed to a naked flame—nor kept in a humid environment, as that will accelerate its deterioration. Store items in a dry, relatively cool atmosphere on open shelves or in a ventilated cabinet and out of direct sunlight. Do not seal pieces in plastic bags.

If the surface shows signs of deterioration such as blooming or fine crazing below the surface, seek the services of a plastics conservator, as it may be possible to slow down the damage. As decaying celluloid can infect other pieces close to it, remove the offending item from your collection and store it elsewhere. It may even become necessary to dispose of the decaying article.

Clean sound pieces with a warm, mild liquid-soap solution applied with cotton wool swabs or a soft cloth—but first carefully remove any old wax or greasy deposits with kerosene (paraffin). Dry with absorbent paper tissue. Do not apply a surface finish to the cleaned plastic.

Casein

Casein is produced from the protein that is found in cow's milk. At the end of the nineteenth century it was discovered that casein treated with formaldehyde formed a moderately water-resistant, translucent, thermosetting plastic. This was produced in a wide range of colors and also used to imitate natural materials such as tortoiseshell and horn.

Most items that are made from casein—such as fountain pens, belt buckles, and hand brushes and hand mirrors, as well as the more common decorative button—are fabricated from solid sections and are not usually molded.

Maintaining casein

Casein will give up and absorb moisture, which can result in fine crazing of the surface. Keep items in a moderate, stable environment and out of direct sunlight. Clean with swabs of very mild liquid-soap solution, then blot dry with absorbent tissue. First test the surface to establish if the colors are fast. If they are not, work on a small area at a time. Seal the surface with a fine film of microcrystalline wax.

Cellulose acetate

Cellulose acetate is based on the same natural polymer as cellulose nitrate, but it uses acetic acid to produce a nonflammable thermoplastic. Its initial applications were similar to celluloid but, with the development of suitable plasticizers in the early part of the twentieth century, it began to be used for the newly developing injection-molding processes. It is a tough material and is widely used for toys in preference to brittle materials such as Bakelite or polystyrene.

When cellulose acetate degrades, it displays signs of white blooming or distortion. It also gives off the vinegary smell of acetic acid. Treat products that are made from cellulose acetate as you would treat celluloid. However, as some have volatile plasticizers that tend to evaporate, causing the object to distort, keep them in a closed, unvented cabinet.

Thermosetting plastics

These are produced as powders for molding into rigid household items and fittings by the application of heat and pressure. Bakelite is arguably the most familiar brand name of this type and was to epitomize the new era of mass-produced plastics. Developed in 1909 in the U.S.A by L.H. Baekeland, a Belgian-American, it was the first solely synthetic-resin plastic. Formed from phenol (a derivative of tar or benzene) and formaldehyde and combined with fillers, it made a hard, stable, strong plastic with excellent electrical and heat-resistant properties.

Bakelite was used for a wide range of domestic products in the electrical-appliance field, particularly molded radio and television cabinets. Most were a dark-brown color, and some were mottled. A casting type of phenol-formaldehyde resin was also produced in translucent form and in a range of colors.

Maintaining Bakelite

Sunlight can cause the surface to dull and loose some of its color, but otherwise the material is not unduly harmed by normal domestic conditions. Clean it with a mild liquid-soap solution applied with a soft cloth, but do not soak it in water. Dry with a soft, clean cloth. If you want to revive the color, use a mildly abrasive car paint cleaner applied with a cloth pad, then wash the plastic again. Protect the surface with a fine coating of microcrystalline wax, if it is appropriate.

Amino plastics

This is the technical term for a range of thermosetting resins that are based on urea and its derivatives combined with formaldehyde. Although they were produced and used in a similar way to phenolic resins (see above), they were made in a wide range of light and dark colors.

The first—marketed under the name Beatl, derived from "Beat All," an advertising slogan—was introduced in the mid-1920s. Urea-formaldehyde and melamine-formaldehyde resins followed—the latter in the mid-1930s. Both were rigid and strong, but melamine had the advantage of having better scratch and heat resistance. Melamine is commonly used for tough, colorful tableware, as well as plastic laminates for work surfaces. Care for amino plastics as you would for Bakelite (see above).

POLYETHYLENE

POLYSTYRENE

Polyvinyl chloride (PVC)

PVC is a synthetic thermoplastic material that is produced by polymerizing vinyl chloride. It is a relatively rigid plastic that can be modified by the use of plasticizers to make a flexible material and by other additives for use in a variety of ways.

The early PVCs of the 1930s were relatively unstable and were produced in film form and as flexible sheet material. Later PVC was combined with fabric to make "leathercloth," and molded to make flexible toys such as soft-faced dolls and squeaky playthings. Its low cost and ability to be molded with fine detail enabled it to become the preferred material for making recording disks.

Modern rigid unplasticized PVC—the development of which began in the 1950s—is now a common material used by the building trade for items, such as window frames and claddings, that were formerly made from wood.

Maintaining PVC

Old PVC products are likely to lose their flexibility due to the loss of plasticizer. Do not flex hardened-plastic items unduly. Keep them out of direct sunlight and in a cool environment. PVC plasticizer may affect other plastics: it will dissolve polystyrene items in contact with it, so store them in separate compartments. Clean dirty surfaces with a mild liquid-soap solution, then dry with a soft cloth. Do not use solvents on plasticized PVC.

PVC

ACRYLIC RESIN

Acrylic-resin plastic

Polymethyl methacrylate, commonly known as Perspex or Plexiglas, is a transparent thermoplastic. Typically produced in sheet or rod form, it is made in a wide range of translucent and opaque colors.

A liquid resin for cold casting is also produced and may be recognized by its use for decorative pieces featuring embedded objects, although in recent times polyester resin has been the preferred material for this purpose.

Developed in the 1930s, sheet acrylic was widely used as a substitute for glass. It was also formed and made into a variety of domestic items. It can be solvent welded and hand polished and is readily worked by ordinary hand tools and machine processes. Moldable acrylics were also made, and were used for such items as buttons and telephone appliances in place of the older Bakelite versions.

AMINO–RESIN
PLASTICS

Maintaining acrylic plastic
Perspex is a stable plastic that weathers well. Clean it with a mild liquid-soap solution, then pat it dry with an absorbent cloth or tissue. Do not rub the surface, since this causes a static charge that will attract dust. However, antistatic cleaners (available from specialist suppliers) provide a protective coating that lasts for a month or more. Avoid the use of solvent cleaners, as these can cause crazing of the polished surface.

The high-gloss surface will easily scratch if it is abraded, so remove surface dust regularly with a soft brush. Fine scratches can be polished out relatively easily (see page 136).

Polyethylene

Polyethylene—or polythene, as it is also called—is a thermoplastic and was first produced in 1933. Derived from ethylene, it is a tough, flexible, waterproof, highly insulative, acid-resistant, and non-toxic plastic. It is made in two basic versions: low-density (which has a soft, greasy feel) and high-density (which is more rigid). It has a translucent gray-blue coloring, but it is also made in a range of opaque and translucent colors. Typical uses include food containers, toys, and novel and decorative household items.

Polystyrene

Polystyrene is a hard, rigid, somewhat brittle, transparent thermoplastic that was made in a wide range of colors. Produced in large quantities in the latter half of the 1930s, it has excellent molding and insulative properties. High-impact grades were introduced in the late 1940s, although they have since been superseded by the modern ABS plastics; they are typically found in opaque colors.

Polystyrene can be injection molded, thermoformed, and extruded. It can also be bonded with a solvent adhesive. It has been widely used in the manufacturing of electrical appliances, household items and toys, and in recent years as foamed insulants and packaging. You can usually identify polystyrene by the tinny metallic sound it makes when it is tapped.

Maintaining polyethylene and polystyrene
Protect old examples from strong light, since these plastics are liable to degrade and their colors fade. Clean with a warm, mild liquid-soap solution. Do not use solvents for cleaning polystyrene.

REPAIRING PLASTIC ARTIFACTS

Generally plastics are not easy materials to work, making attempts at repair difficult. Most plastic artifacts are molded in one piece—but some have separate molded or fabricated components that are assembled with mechanical fixings, such as self-tapping screws, and others may be bonded together.

Most plastics do not glue well, although both thermosets and rigid thermoplastics can usually be bonded with epoxy-resin adhesive. Cyanoacrylate glue (superglue) can also be used for small repairs—although conservators tend not to use it, as the long-term effect of its solvents are not yet known.

Polystyrene and acrylic plastic can be glued with their own solvent adhesive. Polystyrene cement (commonly used for plastic kits) is available from model stores, and acrylic adhesive from suppliers of acrylic plastics. These will produce a strong weldlike bond, but they need to be applied carefully to avoid damaging the surrounding plastic.

Stress cracking

Stress in plastic can be recognized as a light bloom on some plastics and fine crazing in the case of acrylic and polystyrene plastics—an effect that is compounded in the presence of solvents and bonding cements. In severe cases it causes the plastic to break. Stresses can be caused by the molding process, applied pressure, or heat generated by the fabrication processes. Manufacturers of acrylic try to overcome stress problems by a controlled heating and cooling process.

Little can be done once stress damage occurs—but as a general rule to avoid accelerating the problem, do not use solvents to clean plastics. However, lighter fluid or kerosene (paraffin) can be used sparingly to remove sticky gum deposits from all plastics, other than rigid polystyrene, acrylics and flexible PVC.

Mending broken Bakelite

Being relatively brittle, Bakelite can be broken easily if it is struck or dropped. Moldings are usually made with thick walls, enabling the broken edges to be aligned and bonded together in a similar way to ceramics. If it is necessary, use lighter fluid to remove greasy deposits from an old break, then wash the plastic with a warm, liquid-soap solution.

1 Applying glue

Assemble the break without glue to check the fit. Heat the parts slowly with a hair dryer until the plastic is hot to touch. This will encourage the glue to flow into the joint. Apply a thin film of epoxy-resin adhesive, prepared according to the manufacturer's instructions, to the broken edge of the main component. Fit and press in the broken-off piece. Apply strips of self-adhesive tape under tension across the break to hold it together until the glue sets.

2 Trimming the joint

Before the glue is fully cured, peel off the tape and, using the tip of a knife, carefully slice off any excess glue from the break. To avoid marking the polished surface, don't let the blade dig into or scrape the plastic.

3 Filling in chipped edges

If it is necessary after gluing, fill a chipped edge with a colored filler made from ground-up scraps of Bakelite mixed with epoxy-resin adhesive. Clean up the filled surface with a knife (as described above).

Removing scratches

Acrylic plastics (Perspex) have a high-gloss surface that can be marred by scratches. It is possible to remove deep scratches by hand, using fine water-lubricated wet-and-dry abrasive paper, followed by hand polishing (see below). However, it is much easier to use a power buff with a calico mop treated with a mildly abrasive buffing soap. Only use light pressure, to avoid overheating the plastic. Work a larger patch than just the scratch area, to "feather" the edge in order to avoid obvious distortion in the surface.

Polishing by hand

A matt surface caused by fine scratches can be polished out by hand, using proprietary acrylic polishes that are available from plastics suppliers. Alternatively, use a mildly abrasive chrome-polishing cream.

Apply the polish with a soft cloth pad, working in an overlapping circular motion. Finally, buff the surface with a clean, soft cloth.

IDENTIFICATION OF PLASTICS

MATERIAL POPULAR NAME	COLOR	CLARITY	CHARACTERISTICS	FORM	TYPICAL EXAMPLES
HARD RUBBER **EBONITE** **VULCANITE**	Typically black, but also red and ripple mixtures.	Opaque.	Hard. Gives off sulfurous smell if rubbed. Turns brown when exposed to light.	Machine fabricated or molded.	Vesta boxes, combs, fountain pens, and jewelry. Pink ebonite was used for dentures.
SHELLAC **FLORENCE COMPOUND**	Dark brown, black, or red ocher.	Opaque.	Hard and brittle. Smells like sealing wax if melted.	Usually molded.	Decorative picture frames, 78 rpm records, boxes, and union cases.
CELLULOSE NITRATE **CELLULOID** **XYLONITE**	Any color, including mottles, pearls, and special effects.	Transparent, translucent, or opaque.	Flexible and tough. Smells of camphor when warmed by rubbing or warm water.	Usually very thin sheet. Hollow moldings may be filled with plaster to add weight.	Thin covering on mirror backs and other nightstand items. Fountain pens.
CASEIN **ERINOID** **GALALITH**	Any color, including mottles, pearls, and special effects.	Usually opaque, but some translucency when used for mock tortoiseshell and horn.	Hard. Sometimes smells of formaldehyde when placed in water.	Usually machined to shape, sometimes hot-stamped into shallow shapes. Not molded.	Colored knitting needles, buttons, and propelling pencils.
PHENOLIC MOLDING POWDER **BAKELITE**	Usually brown, red, or green mottle or plain black or brown.	Opaque.	Hard and brittle. The surface is often discolored brown and will mark a tissue rubbed against it. May smell of carbolic when warmed.	Always molded into shape.	Radio cabinets, ashtrays, and electrical plugs and sockets.
CAST PHENOLIC RESIN **CATALIN**	Any color is possible, but rarely white or blue.	Often translucent and marbled, seldom transparent, and sometimes opaque.	Hard. The surface is often discolored brown and will mark a tissue rubbed against it. May smell of carbolic when warmed.	Usually cut sections of rod, tube, etc. Often carved.	Animal napkin rings and carved bangles. Also "Carvacraft" deskware and some American radio cabinets.
AMINO PLASTICS **BEATL** **BANDALASTA** **LINGA-LONGA** **BEETLEWARE** **MELAMINE**	Any plain color, but also marbled or speckled.	Never transparent, but can be translucent and sometimes marbled like alabaster. Beetleware may be translucent or opaque. Melamine is opaque.	Hard and brittle like Bakelite, but amino plastics do not discolor with age.	Always molded into shape.	Bandalasta and Linga-longa: colorful, marbled picnicware. Beetleware: pale-colored electrical plugs and sockets. Melamine: tough, colorful tableware.
CELLULOSE ACETATE **ACETATE** **BEXOID**	Any color, usually plain, but occasionally marbled.	Transparent, translucent, or opaque.	Tough and slightly soft, may be flexible in thin sections. Often smells of vinegar, especially when warmed.	Normally molded.	Films, some eyeglasses frames, "Pedigree" dolls, and some toys.
ACRYLIC RESIN **PERSPEX** **PLEXIGLAS**	Any color, but pastel colors were popular.	Transparent, translucent, or opaque.	Hard, not brittle. Smooth glasslike surface that can be scratched easily.	Normally fabricated by hot-shaping from sheet, but can also be molded.	Shallow dishes, lamps, clocks, and transparent brooches with carving on rear.
POLYVINYL CHLORIDE **PVC** **VINYL**	Any color.	Transparent, translucent, or opaque.	Soft and very flexible, though modern PVCs can be rigid and tough. Surface may feel "sticky."	"Leathercloth" coatings or molded.	Flexible, "squeaky" toys, hollow balls, hollow belts, and gramophone records.
POLYSTYRENE **STYRENE**	Any color. Pearl was popular for a while, so were "streaky" color effects.	Transparent, translucent, or opaque.	Hard and brittle, but sometimes toughened. Very "tinny" metallic ring when tapped.	Usually molded.	Toys, self-assembly models, and cheap "giveaways."
POLYETHYLENE **POLYTHENE** **ALKATHENE**	Any color.	Generally translucent, but sometimes opaque.	Soft and flexible. Has greasy feel and can be scratched with fingernail.	Usually molded.	Air-tight food containers, toys and "poppit-bead" necklaces.

Glossary

Where there is more than one term that is commonly used, the second is listed in *bold italics*.

Acetone
Colorless, flammable liquid used as a solvent and cleaning fluid.

Acid-free
Term used to describe a material (usually paper or cardboard manufactured from rag fiber or purified wood pulp) that has a neutral or slightly alkaline pH factor.

Acrylic varnish
Clear, water-based varnish, used primarily as a wood finish or as a protective coating for paintings. It is also used to simulate glaze when restoring ceramics.

Airbrush
Designed to spray paint and other finishes, such as glaze or varnish. An airbrush is capable of extremely precise work.

Alloy
A mixture of two or more metals.

Animal glue
Traditional woodworking adhesive made from animal skin and bones. It is supplied in the form of granules or gel for mixing with hot water.

Banding
Plain or patterned strip of veneer used to make decorative borders. *See also* crossbanding.

Black lead polish
Oil dressing
A mixture of graphite and soft waxes that produces a dark gray metallic sheen on cast iron. Manufactured originally as a grate polish.

Blister
Small raised area of veneer resulting from insufficient glue at that point.

Block
The core of a bound book, comprising leaves of paper sewn and glued together.

Bloom
Cloudy, white stain that appears on clear finishes affected by the ingress of moisture or by the application of heat.

Blueing
The controlled production of a protective film of rich blue oxide that prevents steel from corroding. Blueing is used extensively for gun barrels and for the hands of clocks and watches.

Bodying up
The process of applying successive layers of shellac polish (French polish) to create a film of the required thickness.

Bolt ring
Hollow, circular clasp, incorporating a retractable bolt. Used as a fastening for bracelets and necklaces.

Boulle
Decorative inlay comprising sheet brass and tortoiseshell. Also known as buhl.

Bradawl
Small hand tool for boring holes. It has a sharp screwdriver-like tip that severs the grain, preventing the wood from splitting as the tool is inserted.

Britannia metal
A form of pewter, containing tin, antimony, and copper. It is stronger and lighter in color than "old" pewter and is often used for electroplated metalware.

Brushing French polish
Shellac polish formulated for application with a paintbrush instead of the usual cloth pad.

Buffer
An alkaline substance added to cardboard or paper to ensure that they are acid-free.

Button polish
Superior-quality French polish made nowadays from golden-brown shellac flakes.

Cabochon
Domed, unfaceted stone set into a piece of jewelry.

Came
Grooved strip of lead used to hold the quarries in place in a leaded light or stained-glass window. *See also* quarries.

Cellulose filler
Spackle
Water-based filler used by decorators to patch holes or cracks in plaster. Can also be used as a filler for restoring damaged earthenware.

Chamois leather
Soft suede polishing cloth made from goatskin or sheepskin, also known as a shammy or chammy leather. It was formerly made from the hide of a chamois antelope.

Close grain
Term used to describe fine-textured wood with small, closely spaced cells.

Closed setting
Metal mounting with an enclosed recess for a gemstone.

Crackle glaze
Glaze that is deliberately crazed during the manufacturing process to create a decorative finish for some ceramics.

Crazing
Fine network of cracks found in the glaze of pottery or porcelain.

Crossbanding
Strips of decorative veneer banding with the grain running at right angles to the main axis.

Cut glass
Glassware decorated with facets, deep grooves, and hollows cut by an abrasive wheel.

Cyanoacrylate glue
Clear general-purpose adhesive with an acrylate base. Known commercially as "superglue."

Distilled water
Water that has been distilled commercially to remove impurities.

Document cleaner
Powdered eraser contained in an open-weave bag, used for cleaning soiled paper by gentle abrasion of the surface.

Document-repair tape
Self-adhesive, acid-free paper tape made with reversible acrylic adhesive.

Dust jacket
Removable, printed-paper sleeve wrapped around a bound book.

Earthenware
Opaque, porous pottery, fired at a relatively low temperature, that requires the application of a glaze to make it waterproof. Earthenware has a comparatively thick, coarse-textured body and comes in a variety of colors, ranging from reddish brown to off-white and black.

Ebonized
Stained black to imitate genuine ebony.

Ebony polish
Black-stained French polish used for finishing very dark woods. Ebony polish was traditionally the preferred finish for pianos.

Electroplating
The process of applying a thin coating of metal, such as silver or chromium, onto a base metal by means of electrolysis.

Enamel
Colored opaque or translucent glass fused to a metal base. Intricate patterns are formed by different methods. With cloisonné enamelware, for example, the areas of color are

separated by flattened metal wire soldered to the base. The base itself is engraved for champlevé enameling, and the resulting hollows are filled in with enamel.

Endpaper
The sheet of paper glued to the inside of the board cover at the front and back of a bound book. One half of the endpaper forms the flyleaf.

Epergne
Ornamental centerpiece for a table. Usually designed to hold flowers or fruits.

Ephemera
Collectable items, such as tickets, labels, and posters, originally not intended to last for more than a short time.

EPNS
Electroplated nickel silver. *See also* nickel silver.

Epoxy-resin glue
Two-part adhesive comprising an epoxy resin and a hardener. When the two are mixed together, the resulting chemical reaction produces a strong, insoluble bond.

Epoxy putty
A two-part filler or modeling compound that sets hard when the two components are kneaded together.

Faience
Tin-glazed earthenware.

Feathering
The action of creating an indiscernible edge to a coat of paint or varnish by blending it into the background color.

Figure
The pattern of grain on the surface of a piece of solid wood or veneer.

Flats
Short for flat figures. Flats are usually cast-metal model soldiers in low-relief, around ¼ inch (2mm) thick.

Flux
Substance used to clean the surfaces of metals before soldering.

Flyleaf
The free half of an endpaper. The first and the last leaf of a bound book are flyleaves.

Folder
Narrow bone spatula used by bookbinders to rub sharp creases into folded paper. Also used for burnishing down adhesive tapes and glued paper.

Foxing
Small brown spots caused by spores growing on the surface of damp paper.

Frass
Fine wood dust created by the activity of wood-boring insects.

French polish
Wood finish made by dissolving shellac in alcohol, applied with a pad of wadding wrapped in cotton or linen cloth. *See also* brushing French polish, button polish, ebony polish, garnet polish, transparent polish, white polish.

Fumed silica
Finely powdered silica used as a matting agent.

Garnet polish
Deep reddish-brown French polish, sometimes used to enhance the color of mahogany and similar woods.

Gelatine
Fine powder prepared by boiling specially prepared animal skin and bones. When mixed with water, gelatine is an excellent paper size.

German silver
See nickel silver.

Gesso
Paste made from rabbit-skin glue and chalk. When applied to wood, it can be sanded to a smooth base for gilding with gold leaf. Colored gesso is sometimes called bole.

Gilding
The process for applying gold leaf or gilt varnish.

Glaze
Hard, glassy, transparent coating applied to ceramics to make them waterproof and for decorative purposes.

Glue starvation
Describes a condition where insufficient glue has been applied to veneer groundwork or woodworking joints, resulting in a breakdown of the bond.

Gold leaf
Wafer-thin sheets of pure gold applied to a surface as a decorative finish. Metal leaf, made from brass, is a cheap substitute.

Grain
The general direction or arrangement of the fibrous material in wood, *or* the direction of the warp and weft threads in woven textiles.

Grain filler
Thin paste used to fill in the open pores of wood prior to applying a glossy wood finish such as French polish.

Groundwork
The backing material, either solid wood or man-made boards, to which veneers are applied.

Hairline crack
Barely visible crack in porcelain or earthenware.

Hard-paste porcelain
A mixture of kaolin (china clay) and petuntse (china stone), hard-paste porcelain originated in China around AD 900. Bone china, made with animal-bone ash, is the standard English and American hard-paste porcelain.

Hard-solder
To make a strong joint between two metal surfaces by fusing a layer of brass or a high-melt solder between them. The process is also known as brazing.

Headband
Narrow cloth band attached to the top and sometimes also to the bottom of the spine of a book.

Hinges
See joints.

Hydrogen peroxide
Bleaching agent available in volume strengths.

Hygroscopic
Having a tendency to absorb moisture from the air.

Inlay
To insert pieces of wood, metal, or semiprecious materials into prepared recesses, so that the materials lie flush with the surrounding surfaces, *or* the piece of inlaid wood, metal, or semiprecious material itself.

Intaglio
Incised carving in the surface of a stone or seal.

Japanning
Glossy finish in imitation of Oriental lacquer.

Joints
The two hinges between a book block and its board covers, formed by a strip of mull reinforced with tapes and covered by endpapers.

Jump ring
Openable metal link at each end of a chain for attaching a clasp or bolt ring.

Karat
Carat
Unit used to measure the purity of precious metals and the weight of gemstones.

Key
To abrade or incise a surface to provide a better grip when gluing something to it or in order to create a strong bond between the surface and a finish such as paint or varnish.

Kilim
Woven rug with no pile, manufactured mostly in the Middle East.

Laying off
Using upward strokes of the brush to blend in the wet edges when finishing an application of paint or varnish.

Leaded light
Window panel made from quarries (small pieces of clear, colored, or textured glass) held in a matrix of narrow lead strips known as cames.

Lime scale
White deposit of mineral salts contained in hard water.

Lipping
Protective strip of solid wood applied to the edge of a panel or tabletop.

Lot
Single item or group of items offered for sale at an auction.

Luster glazes
Metallic finishes for ceramics produced by adding appropriate salts to the glaze.

Lusters
Drop-shaped pieces of glass or crystal hung from chandeliers, lamps, and candlesticks to reflect the light.

Man-made boards
Stable panels manufactured from veneer or wood particles bonded together under pressure.

Marquetry
Relatively small pieces of veneer laid together to make decorative motifs or patterns. *See also* parquetry.

Masking tape
Low-tack self-adhesive tape used primarily to mask and protect areas surrounding surfaces that are to be painted.

Mazac
Alloy of magnesium and zinc used for making die-cast toys.

Methylated spirit
Denatured alcohol
Alcohol that has been denatured by the addition of methanol and pyradine. Often colored with a violet dye, it is used as a solvent, thinner, and cleaning agent. Also known as meths.

Microcrystalline wax
Light, white wax polish used as a dressing for a variety of materials.

Mull
Light open-weave muslin fabric glued to the inner spine of the binding of a book. It forms a major component of the joints between the book block and board covers.

Nacre
Mother-of-pearl. The hard iridescent substance that forms the inner layer of certain mollusk shells.

Nickel silver
Nickel silver, an alloy of copper, zinc, and nickel also known as German silver, is used as the base for plated silverware marked EPNS (electroplated nickel silver).

Niello
Decorative technique for metalware. It consists of a black compound of silver and sulfur with lead or copper, fused into an incised design or pattern.

Open setting
Metal mounting that holds a gemstone in place, but which is open at the back to admit light.

Ormolu
Gilded cast bronze or brass, used for ornaments and for decorative mounts applied to furniture, clocks, and sometimes ceramics.

Oxalic acid
Toxic crystalline dicarboxylic acid, used as a bleaching agent.

Paraffin
Kerosene
Thin fuel oil distilled from petroleum, used as a solvent and cleaning agent.

Parian ware
White, unglazed porcelain, often used for figurines because of its resemblance to marble.

Parquetry
A process similar to marquetry, but using veneers cut into geometric shapes to make decorative patterns.

Patina
Surface coloring and texture produced by a combination of natural ageing and long-term use.

Pile
Texture produced by the cut ends of knotted yarns used to make rugs and carpets.

Pinchbeck
Named after its creator Christopher Pinchbeck, an eighteenth-century watchmaker, this alloy of zinc and copper was made to imitate gold. Used for cheap jewelry, it had gone out of fashion by the mid-nineteenth century.

Planish
To produce a finished surface on metalwork by light hammering.

Plate
An individual printed picture used as a book illustration.

Plating
See electroplating.

Polishing pad
Soft pad used for applying French polish, made from a handful of cotton wadding wrapped in a square of linen or cotton cloth.

Polyethylene
Polymerized ethylene resin used to manufacture protective sheeting and packaging. Also known as polythene.

Porcelain
The fine, white vitrified body of porcelain is created by high-temperature firing. It is extremely hard yet translucent. *See also* hard-paste porcelain and soft-paste porcelain.

PVA adhesive
White glue
Ready-mixed, water-based woodworking glue. A conservation grade is used by bookbinders for repairing books.

Quarries
The individual pieces of glass in leaded lights and stained-glass windows.

Restringing
The process of replacing a worn or broken necklace thread.

Reversible
Describes a process that can be undone easily and which does not have a lasting effect on the piece being worked on.

Rivet
Metal staple used for reinforcing repaired ceramics.

Ruler
Strip of metal or wood machined with at least one true edge, used to mark and cut straight lines and to gauge flat surfaces.

Sealer coat
An application of diluted finish applied to bare wood to prevent subsequent full-strength coats from soaking in.

Section
Part of a bound book comprising a single sheet of paper folded, trimmed, and sewn to create a number of individual leaves.

Sgraffito
Form of decoration used on ceramics. Sgraffito is created by scratching through the slip to expose the ceramic body beneath.

Sheffield plate
Thin rolled-sheet material consisting of silver fused to a copper backing. One or both sides may be plated.

Shell chip
Small, semicircular chip, a common defect on the rim of cups, plates, vases, and other ceramic items.

Shellac
Derived from the resin excreted by the insect *Laccifer lacca*, shellac is dissolved in industrial alcohol to make French polish. Shellac has many other uses, including the production of sanding sealer and sealing wax.

Short grain
Describes where the general direction of wood fibers lies across a narrow section of timber.

Silicon-carbide paper
Sandpaper manufactured from grains of black to dark gray silicon-carbide attached to a paper backing with waterproof glue. Known as wet-and-dry paper, it is used with water as a lubricant for rubbing down coats of paint or varnish. A pale gray silicon-carbide paper coated with a dry powdered lubricant is used for rubbing down finishes that would be harmed by water.

Silver cloth
Polishing cloth impregnated with non-abrasive metal polish for cleaning silver items.

Silver gilt
Silver covered with a thin film of gold.

Slip
Clay mixed with water to a creamy consistency, used for decorating ceramic pieces.

Soft-paste porcelain
With its slightly granular texture, soft-paste porcelain was the result of early European attempts to copy Chinese porcelain.

Soft solder
To join two metal surfaces together using low-melt solder applied with a heated soldering iron.

Spelter
Alloy of copper and zinc used for decorative wares and as a substitute for bronze in the manufacture of cast statues.

Spine
The bound edge of a book.

Sprue
Waste plastic or metal that solidifies in the access channels in casting mlds.

Stained glass
Leaded lights containing painted-glass quarries.

Stainless steel
Relatively modern silver-colored, rust-resistant alloy of steel and chromium.

Stake
Stout piece of wood or metal bar used to back up an item when shaping or planishing metalware.

Stoneware
Hard ceramic with a coarse, granular texture, made by adding flint or stone dust to the clay. Increasing the temperature of the kiln fuses the body and glaze, making it non-porous and harder than low-fired earthenware. Stoneware is usually white, light-brown, or beige in color. Black basalt ware and blue jasper ware are exceptions.

Stove-enameling glaze
Transparent glaze that sets in a relatively low temperature in a domestic oven. It is specially formulated for recoating restored ceramics.

Stringing
A narrow strip of wood used to divide areas of veneer.

Sumak
Type of flat-woven rug from the Caucasus and northwest Persia.

Tacking iron
Thermostatically controlled tool with an electrically heated tip. Used by paper conservators and bookbinders to apply heat-set tissue (tissue paper coated with dry adhesive).

Tarnished
Lightly corroded.

Thinner
Substance used to reduce the consistency of paint, varnish, or polish.

Tinning
Coating the tip of a soldering iron with molten solder.

Tinplate
Thin rolled-steel sheet plated on both sides with tin.

Tipped in
Lightly glued into a book.

Titanium dioxide
White pigment used as an additive in glue to reduce its tendency to turn yellow.

Transparent polish
Practically clear French polish that hardly changes the natural color of wood.

Turpentine
Short for spirits of turpentine. A colorless, oily liquid with a pungent odor, used as a solvent for paint and varnish.

Veneer
Thin slice of wood used as a surface covering on less costly materials such as pine or man-made boards.

Veneer hammer
Tool with a narrow brass strip mounted in its head, used to apply firm pressure when gluing veneer by hand.

Verdigris
Green deposit on brass, copper, or bronze produced by corrosion.

Warp
The longitudinal foundation threads of a woven fabric, *or* to twist or cause to twist out of shape as a result of moisture or heat.

Water stain
Gray or brown stain caused by moisture drawing dirt and other impurities into the fibers of cloth or paper.

Weft
The transverse threads of woven fabric. Weft threads weave over and under warp threads.

Weld
To fuse together two pieces of metal or plastic by the application of heat or pressure. When welding metal, it is normal to apply additional molten metal to the joint. With plastic, a solvent is often applied to the joining surface.

Wet-and-dry paper
See silicon-carbide paper.

White polish
Milky-white variety of French polish made from bleached shellac. It is used for finishing pale colored woods.

White spirit
Mineral spirits
Colorless solvent obtained from petroleum, used as a thinner for paints and varnishes. Also known as turpentine substitute.

Window mount
Piece of cardbard with a rectangular aperture, commonly used when framing pictures behind glass.

Wire wool
Steel wool
Mass of fine steel strands, used for smoothing surfaces and applying finishes.

Woodworm
Larvae of the furniture beetle that feed on wood fibers, leaving an intricate network of fine tunnels in the timber.

INDEX